Financial Inclusion and Beyond

Published by Academic Foundation
in association with

Justice K.S. Hegde Institute of Management, Nitte

<u>About the Authors</u>

N.K. Thingalaya is the Chairman of the Academic Council of Justice K.S. Hegde Institute of Management (JKSHIM), Nitte, with teaching and research interests in banking and microfinance and rural development. He has a doctoral degree in economics from the University of Bombay. Dr. Thingalaya has been a member of the Planning Board of the Government of Karnataka, is the former Chairman and Managing Director of Syndicate Bank and has been member of several committees appointed by the Reserve Bank of India. He was the Chairman of the Working Group in Microfinance constituted for preparation of the Eleventh Five-Year Plan.

M.S. Moodithaya is the Director and Professor in international business at JKSHIM. A postgraduate in cost accounting from the University of Mysore, he received his doctoral degree from the Mangalore University and postgraduate diploma in marketing and sales management from Bharatiya Vidya Bhavan, Bombay. He has more than twenty-five years of teaching, research and industrial experience.

N.S. Shetty is Professor Emeritus at JKSHIM. He is an Agricultural Economist with a doctoral degree from University of Bombay. Dr. Shetty has prepared a number of policy documents and study reports for different agencies. He has produced many research publications on various issues relating to agricultural economics particularly with a global perspective. He takes keen interest in the developments in African and European continents.

Financial Inclusion and Beyond

Issues and Challenges

N.K. Thingalaya

M.S. Moodithaya

N.S. Shetty

ACADEMIC FOUNDATION

NEW DELHI

First published in 2010
by

ACADEMIC FOUNDATION
4772-73 / 23 Bharat Ram Road, (23 Ansari Road),
Darya Ganj, New Delhi - 110 002 (India).
Phones : 23245001 / 02 / 03 / 04.
Fax : +91-11-23245005.
E-mail : books@academicfoundation.com
www. academicfoundation.com

in association with

Justice K.S. Hegde Institute of Management, Nitte

Cataloging in Publication Data--DK
  Courtesy: D.K. Agencies (P) Ltd. <docinfo@dkagencies.com>

Thingalaya, N. K., 1937-
  Financial inclusion and beyond : issues and challenges /
N.K. Thingalaya, M.S. Moodithaya, N.S. Shetty.
     p.   cm.
In Indian context.
Includes bibliographical references (p.   ).
  ISBN 13: 9788171888351
  ISBN 10: 8171888356

  1. Rural credit--India. 2. Banks and banking--India. 3.
Financial services industry--India.   I. Moodithaya, M. S., joint
author. II. Shetty, N. S., joint author. III. Title.

DDC 332.710954   22

Typeset and cover design: Italics India, New Delhi.

Printed and bound in India.

Contents

List of Tables, Boxes and Annexures

Tables

Boxes

Annexures

डॉ. सी. रगंराजन
Dr. C. RANGARAJAN

अध्यक्ष
प्रधानमंत्री की आर्थिक सलाहकार परिषद्
विज्ञान भवन सौंध 'ई' हाल
मौलाना आज़ाद रोड
नई दिल्ली—110 011
CHAIRMAN
Economic Advisory Council to the Prime Minister
Vigyan Bhavan Annexe, 'E' Hall
Maulana Azad Road
New Delhi-110 011

July 20, 2010

Foreword

I am happy to write the Foreword for the book "Financial Inclusion and Beyond: Issues and Challenges". The authors—N.K. Thingalaya, M.S. Moodithaya and N.S. Shetty—have written an extremely useful book on the subject of financial inclusion. It is very timely as the subject is being hotly discussed among the policymakers and the academics. The authors have rich background in banking and finance. They are also deeply committed to the cause of rural banking.

Access to finance by the poor and vulnerable groups is a pre-requisite for poverty reduction. Truly speaking, providing access to finance is a form of empowerment of vulnerable groups. Financial inclusion denotes delivery of financial services at an affordable cost to the vast segments of disadvantaged and low income groups. Financial inclusion aims at extending the scope of activities of the organised financial system to include within its ambit people with low incomes. Through the provision of financial services, an attempt is made to lift the poor from one level to another so that they come out of poverty. Policy initiatives aimed at financial inclusion have been studied by several committees including the Committee on Financial Inclusion which was chaired by me.

दूरभाष: 011-23022311, 23022313 फ़ैक्स: 011-23022318 ई-मेल: c.rangarajan@nic.in
Telephone: 011-23022311, 23022313 Fax: 011-23022318 e-mail: c.rangarajan@nic.in

This book looks at the various dimensions of financial inclusion and comes up with interesting new ideas on how to achieve this goal. The authors have also studied the way financial exclusion operates at the ground level through a survey of certain villages and households in the four southern states. The survey provides insights into the nature of exclusion. The book includes an interesting analysis of the various initiatives on financial inclusion. There is a meaningful discussion of the Self Help Groups which is regarded by many as an important instrument for achieving financial inclusion. As the way ahead the authors advocate extending the service points, setting up Gramin Vikas Soudhas and reorienting Lead Bank Scheme. These are useful suggestions stemming from rich banking experience.

The country has moved to a higher growth trajectory. But it is equally necessary to ensure that the benefits of growth reach everyone. Financial inclusion of hitherto excluded segments of population is a critical part of the process of inclusive growth. The chief merit of the book is that it provides a roadmap for achieving the goal of financial inclusion.

(C. Rangarajan)

Preface

The major thrust of this book is evolving a workable model for purposeful financial inclusion, which can be adopted by banks and other financial institutions. It is based on a study which has relied both on secondary data and primary data covering villages from four states of South India namely, Andhra Pradesh, Karnataka, Kerala and Tamil Nadu. A comprehensive evaluation of the macro level data relating to the evolution and growth of banking services in the state and districts selected were made, based on secondary data published by the Reserve Bank of India, concerned banks and various other published and semi-published sources. Besides, data was also collected relating to the socio-economic conditions of the states and districts covered under the study. Interactions with rural branch managers, NGOs and selected SHGs were done at various levels. For primary data collection at village level from the households, a structured questionnaire was designed and used. Personal interactions were held with officials engaged in provision of financial services at the village level. Based on the study, several policy implications for redrawing the procedure in vogue for improving the effectiveness of the financial inclusion programmes are made. The role of various agencies involved in this process are critically evaluated and clearly demarcated for their effective performance in this area.

The book is divided into nine chapters. While Chapter 1, deals with the introductory background with technical details of the study, Chapter 2 provides a conceptual framework for the study. It also adumbrates various dimensions of financial exclusion, factors affecting financial inclusion and strategies adopted in various countries as a backdrop. An assessment of financial inclusion and exclusion in India based on secondary data is carried out in depth in Chapter 3. Earlier approaches for financial inclusion and recent initiatives are discussed in detail, in Chapters 4 and 5. Since the study focuses on the developments in the sphere of financial inclusion in the southern states, Chapter 6 makes an analysis of the current status of banking and provides a profile of banking facilities in the districts selected. Based on the field study, in Chapter 7, an attempt is made to determine the extent of financial inclusion and exclusion, problems of access to financial services, socioeconomic profile of financially included and financially excluded households and factors determining financial inclusion at the household level. Chapter 8 provides an account of the actions initiated by various banks in response to the recent directives by Reserve Bank of India on financial inclusion. The last chapter provides a glimpse into the way forward with appropriate recommendations for achieving 100 per cent financial inclusion.

The study concludes that the objective of making financial inclusion a success, in the real sense cannot be achieved in a year or two. The achievement should be made in a phased manner with a time horizon dictated by clear-cut goals and action plans by taking into account the specific local conditions. On the way forward, the real challenge is for the banks and other financial institutions to adopt ICT solutions and multiple channels for expanding outreach and delivery of variety of financial products and services at affordable costs on sustainable basis. This requires attitudinal change, change in organisational structure and innovative models of delivery at the doorstep of poor and weaker sections of the society. As rightly pointed out by Rangarajan Committee, financial inclusion is no longer an option; it is a compulsion.

M.S. Moodithaya
N.K. Thingalaya
N.S. Shetty

1 Introduction

The banking sector in India has undergone far reaching changes in terms of coverage, credit disbursement and banking technology in providing the banking services during the last four decades. The nationalisation of 14 commercial banks in 1969 was a major landmark in the journey of Indian banking towards mass banking from class banking. Remarkable progress was made in extending banking facilities, mitigating to some extent the regional inequalities in the availability of banking services. Thousands of new banking centres even in remote villages started appearing on the banking map of the country. Institutional innovations in rural credit delivery system were introduced. But it was realised that the banking system is yet to reach a wide section of the population both in rural and urban areas.

With the opening of branches both in rural and urban centres, the number of bank customers has increased substantially. The number of savings bank accounts has increased from 2.36 crore in 1971, to 42.91 crore as on March 2008, according to the latest data available. The total number of deposit accounts is 58.16 crore. While the urban and metropolitan branches have 18.29 crore savings bank accounts, the rural branches handle 13.30 crore accounts and semi-urban branches have 11.32 crore accounts (RBI, 2009).

The number of borrowing accounts also has increased very impressively during this period, though not as rapidly as the deposit accounts. The number of small borrowing accounts—amount borrowed being less than Rs.10,000—was only 10.02 lakh in 1968. It has gone up to 9.45 crore in 2008 (The cut-off level for small borrowing is now Rs.25,000). The total number of borrowing accounts now stands at 10.70 crore. The actual number of bank borrowers would be much lower than this figure, as many borrowers invariably have more than one borrowing account. The number of borrowing accounts handled by banks in rural India is again much lower, 3.04 crore only. Considering the growing population, the number of people who remain unreached as bank borrowers could be certainly larger than those reached so far.

The development that has taken place in the Indian banking sector since nationalisation could be equated with voiceless growth. The deprived are too many, but too poor to assert. They are voiceless, suffering silently, resigned to their fate. It is a sad commentary on the inability of the banking sector that even after nearly four decades of public sector banking or directed banking, it could not contribute to the empowerment of the masses, who are excluded from reaping the benefits of banking development. The banking system has not been successful in replacing the omnipotent moneylender. Millions of poor farmers, who borrow from moneylenders, are in double jeopardy, as they are paying very high interest rates and are not getting any debt relief, which was recently announced in the Union Budget of 2009-10.

According to the All India Debt and Investment Survey 2002, moneylender's share in the debt of rural households has gone up from 17.5 per cent in 1991 to 29.6 per cent in 2002. More disheartening is the decline in the share of commercial banks during the same period; from 33.7 per cent to 24.5 per cent. No serious attempts have been made to consolidate the banking system so as to develop a strong alternative to the moneylender. The large number of highly indebted farmers committing suicide in different states came as an eye-opener for the planners and policymakers that the institutional credit agencies in the country are not sensitised enough to safeguard the interests of poor farmers.

Some very interesting data relating to the extent to which the banking services have percolated into the households in different parts of the country are available in the Census of India publication *Analytical Report on Household Assets.* Census 2001, for the first time, has generated authentic data relating to the number of households in India availing banking services. The definition used here is "The household was considered availing banking services, if its head and or any other member in the household were availing banking services provided by the bank or post office bank as a holder of any type of bank account. This covers all types of commercial banks such as nationalised banks, private banks, foreign banks and the cooperative banks". A household is "usually a group of persons, who normally live together and take their meal from a common kitchen, unless the exigencies of work prevent any of them from doing so" (Census, 2008).

According to this source, out of 13.83 crore rural households in India, only 4.16 crore households (30.11 per cent) have availed banking services. If 30.11 per cent is considered as the rural penetration ratio, wide variations could be seen in it across the states; varying from 6 per cent in Manipur to 56 per cent in Uttarakhand. At the national level, the urban penetration ratio is 49.52 per cent. It reaches the highest level in Goa (77 per cent). The average penetration ratio for rural and urban population works out to be 35.54 per cent. It implies that over 12 crore households in India, of whom more than 9 crore live in rural India, are yet to be touched by banks.

Recent Thrust on Financial Inclusion

The Governor of Reserve Bank of India in the Annual Policy Statement for 2006-07 announced two of the major policy prescriptions relating to the need for improving the rural credit delivery mechanism. Recognising the need for enlarging the coverage of rural households and enhancing the scope and content of rural credit, banks have been advised to initiate action in these areas. Achieving 100 per cent financial inclusion in at least one district in each state and the formation of grassroot level agency for counseling the debt-ridden farmers in distress were the two significant programmes emerging from this policy statement.

For initiating the necessary steps to achieve financial inclusion, in the policy statement it was announced, "SLBC conveners in all states and union territories would be advised to identify at least one district in their area for achieving 100 per cent financial inclusion by providing a 'no-frills' account and a general purpose credit card (GCC) on the lines of the initiative taken in Pondicherry". Since then, banks have been directed to extend their services to ensure 100 per cent financial inclusions, at least in some selected districts to begin with.

Banks embarked upon a massive programme for reaching out to the hitherto unreached persons by opening their savings bank accounts. To hasten the process of enrolling new customers, banks relaxed the rules relating to the minimum amount of money to be initially deposited and also the stipulation pertaining to the minimum balance to be maintained in the account. Zero balance savings bank accounts were introduced by banks, some of which were mercilessly charging earlier a fine for defaults in maintaining minimum balance.

Committee on Financial Inclusion

The Government of India constituted a Committee on Financial Inclusion under the chairmanship of Dr. C. Rangarajan on June 26, 2006, and its final report was submitted in January 2008. This Committee has defined financial inclusion as "the process of ensuring access to financial services and timely and adequate credit where needed by vulnerable groups such as weaker sections and low income groups at an affordable cost".

With a view to achieve financial inclusion in a holistic manner, it is essential to ensure that a range of financial services is available to every household. These services are:

- Opening no-frills banking account for making and receiving payments.
- Operating savings bank accounts suited to the poor households.
- Offering money transfer facilities.
- Extending small loans for productive, personal and other purposes.
- Providing micro-insurance (life and non-life).

Opening a savings bank account is the first step in introducing individuals into the banks. Illiteracy and lack of awareness of banking transactions, coupled with meagre income, almost compel the rural poor to remain away from the banks. And often the banks also do not care to initiate steps to bring such people to the banking fold. It is therefore suggested that the banks should open no-frills accounts with very little amount of minimum opening balance or zero balance. 'No-frills' banking accounts enable the account holder to receive and make payments through the bank. The operational conditions of the savings bank account should be suited to the pattern of cash flows of a poor household. Money transfer facility is one of the common facilities used by all households to remit money to their villages or to children studying in cities. Extension of small loans for productive purposes or for personal needs is one of the most essential ingredients of financial inclusion. Providing micro-insurance, both life and non-life, is another very important service banks can undertake in the rural areas.

The recommendations of the Committee include the following:

1. Launching of a National Rural Financial Inclusion Plan (NRFIP) in mission mode with a clear target to provide access to comprehensive financial services, including credit, to at least 50 per cent (say 55.77 million) of the financially excluded rural cultivator/non-cultivator households, by 2012 through rural/semi-urban branches of commercial banks and regional rural banks. The remaining households have to be covered by 2015.

2. For the purpose, a National Mission on Financial Inclusion (NaMFI) is proposed to be constituted comprising representatives from all stakeholders to aim at achieving universal financial inclusion within a specific timeframe.

3. Constitution of two funds with NABARD:

   - Financial Inclusion Promotion and Development Fund (FIPF). This fund will focus on interventions like, "farmers' service centres", "promoting rural entrepreneurship", "self-help groups and their federations", "developing human resources of banks", "promotion of resource centres" and "capacity building of business facilitators and correspondents".

   - Financial Inclusion Technology Fund (FITF) with an initial corpus of Rs.500 crore each to be contributed by Government of India/RBI/NABARD. This fund will focus on funding of low-cost technology solutions. (This recommendation has already been accepted by Government of India.)

4. Deepening the outreach of microfinance programme through financing of SHG/JLGs (Joint Liability Groups) and setting up of a risk mitigation mechanism for lending to small marginal farmers/share croppers/tenant farmers through JLG.

Targets for Inclusive Growth

The commercial banks, regional rural banks and the cooperative banks are charged with the responsibility of achieving 100 per cent financial inclusion by 2012. During the next three years, at least 50 per cent of the financially excluded rural cultivator/non-cultivator households should be covered by extending credit facilities. The remaining households are to be covered by 2015.

For operationalising these targets, it is spelt out in the Report that "semi-urban and rural branches of commercial banks and RRBs should cover a minimum of 250 new cultivator and non-cultivator households per branch per annum." The Report has adopted a target-oriented approach to achieve financial inclusion, without insisting upon an integrated approach to be adopted at the village level by banks, based on the aspirations and expectations of the rural households.

Responding to the need for achieving financial inclusion, though belatedly, the bankers have started moving and some are moving very fast. Even before estimating the gravity of the situation, a few of them have declared the achievement of 100 per cent financial inclusion, adopting the route of no-frills accounts in the selected districts. What could not be accomplished in four decades cannot be achieved in such a short time.

Operational Importance of the Study

India being a large country, known for its geographic and socioeconomic diversities, there is enough scope for many agencies to operate at different degrees of efficiency and sophistication. Poverty here is a too deep-rooted malady to be removed in a decade or so. The action programmes for poverty eradication go on. The base of the pyramid of wealth is expanding and its peak is growing at a much faster rate, reaching dizzy heights. Yet, it is also now being increasingly recognised that there is fortune at the bottom of the pyramid. Financial inclusion is one such programme aiming at sharing the fortune by all those who subsist under the pyramid. It should not turn out to be fortune hunting process by the greedy players.

The major thrust of the present study is to evolve a workable model for purposeful financial inclusion, which can be adopted by banks. It is an action-oriented project, replicable and useful.

The following are the specific research areas addressed in this study:

1. Making an evaluation of the banking penetration achieved so far.

2. Assessing the effectiveness of various programmes implemented to improve financial inclusion.

3. Evolving a framework for credit mapping for financial inclusion at the village level.

4. Examining the efficacy of SHG movement and microfinance interventions as instruments of financial inclusion.

5. Formulating an integrated model for financial inclusion for the villages selected.

6. Devising a monitoring mechanism for periodical reviews.

7. Recommendations for strategies and policies to look beyond financial inclusion.

The study covers four states of South India namely, Karnataka, Kerala, Tamil Nadu and Andhra Pradesh. It may be noted here that these states have a fairly well-developed banking system. For a detailed study, one district from each of the states is selected. Since the study aims at looking at the strategies to be worked out to look beyond financial inclusion, the relatively better-banked districts of the states are selected. These districts have the wide presence of regional rural banks, rural branches of commercial banks, insurance penetration and SHG networks.

One village from each district is selected for the in-depth study of the process of financial inclusion. The villages selected are of varying socioeconomic backgrounds. All the households in the villages are surveyed with a specially designed structured questionnaire.

The chapters to follow in the book throw light on the different dimensions of financial inclusion, with an emphasis on arriving at an appropriate plan of action for not only reaching out to the unreached, but also making the attempt of reaching out the worthwhile. As, worldwide, the issue of financial inclusion is considered to be one of the prerequisites for attaining the objective of inclusive growth, this study provides enough insights in to the measures to be adopted for reaching this goal. Evidently, financial institutions have to go a long way in using financial inclusion as an instrument for socio-economic empowerment of the poor and the marginalised.

2 | Financial Inclusion

Conceptual Framework

Financial inclusion has recently become the buzzword among the policymakers and bankers and in academic research. It is considered as an integral part of the efforts to promote inclusive economic growth. Access to safe, easy and affordable financial services for poor, vulnerable groups, disadvantaged areas and lagging sectors is a *sine qua non* for accelerated growth and for reducing income disparities and poverty. In fact, access to affordable finance enables the poor and vulnerable groups to undertake economic activities and to take advantage of growth opportunities for economic empowerment. Hence, developing an inclusive financial system to provide equal opportunities to all in accessing financial services at affordable costs is a precondition for achieving accelerated economic growth along with a reduction in income inequality and poverty. Without an inclusive financial system, poor and vulnerable section of the community and small and petty enterprises would not be in a position to take advantages of growth opportunities.

A clearer definition and understanding the various dimensions of financial inclusion is, therefore, considered crucial for identifying the underlying factors that lead to financial exclusion and developing an appropriate policy framework for policy intervention. In this chapter, an attempt is made to look into the conceptual and measurement problems involved in providing a broad framework to empirically examine the nature and various dimensions of financial inclusion or exclusion in the provision of financial services. Based on the conceptual framework, an attempt is also made to identify the factors contributing to financial inclusion and strategies adopted in different countries as a backdrop for the study.

Concept and Definition

Financial services or products provided by banks, finance companies, postal saving banks, credit unions, insurance companies and micro-finance institutions and other formal financial institutions generally form the basis for financial inclusion. The financial services rendered by the informal sources such as moneylenders, traders etc., do not come under the purview of financial inclusion as they are limited in supply and exploitative in nature. The formal financial institutions help mobilise savings and efficient allocation of funds for development. In addition, they provide payment services that facilitate the exchange of goods and services. Efficient and well-functioning financial institutions are, thus, crucial in channeling funds to the most productive uses and thereby boosting economic growth.

Despite critical importance of access to financial services for achieving equitable economic development, in most developing countries, a large segment of the population particularly low income and vulnerable section of the society has very little or no access to financial services from formal financial system. It is estimated that globally over two billion people are currently excluded from the access to financial services (UN, 2006). They normally depend on their own limited resources or informal sources of finance at exorbitantly exploitative terms. Unless the financial system is inclusive, the benefit of financial services is likely to elude many individuals and enterprises and thereby, denying much of the population the benefit of growth opportunities.[1]

Inclusive finance, including safe saving, appropriately designed and at affordable cost loans for poor and low-income households and micro, small and medium sized enterprises and appropriate insurance and payment services can help people to enhance incomes, acquire capital, manage risks and come out of poverty (UN, 2006). Inclusive finance, however, does not mean that everyone who is eligible uses each of these services, but they should be in a position to use them if they so desired.

---

1. UN Secretary-General Kofi Annan declared following the adoption of 2005 as the International Year of Microcredit, "The stark reality is that most poor people in the world will lack access to sustainable financial services, whether it is savings, credit or insurance. The great challenge before us is to address the constraints that exclude people from full participation in the financial sector."

The essence of financial inclusion is, thus, to ensure that a range of appropriate financial services rendered by the formal financial system is available to every individual and enable them to access those services whenever needed. The range of financial services include the entire gamut of financial products—cheque accounts, saving products, loans, debit cards, credit cards, insurance and health care services and other financial services such as payment services, remittance and money transfer and financial advisory services and counseling (Figure 2.1).

Figure 2.1

Financial Inclusion

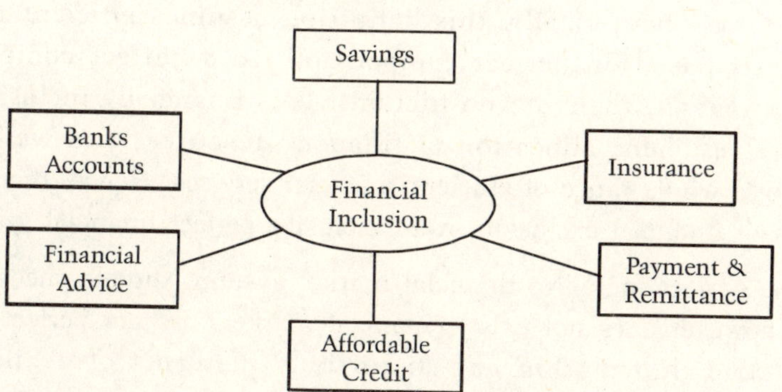

By virtue of the above conceptual framework and with a view to significantly increase outreach to unserved and underserved enterprises and households, the vision of inclusive financial system would be characterised by:

a) Access at reasonable cost of all households and enterprises to the range of financial services for which they are 'bankable' including savings, credit, leasing and factoring, mortgages, insurance, pensions, payments and local and international transfers.

b) Sound institutions guided by appropriate internal management systems, industry performance standards and performance monitoring by the market, as well as by sound prudential regulation where required.

c) Financial and institutional sustainability as a means of providing access to financial services over time, and

d) Multiple providers of financial services, so as to bring cost-effective and a wide variety of alternatives to customers (UN, 2006).

A review of literature reveals that there is no universally accepted definition of financial inclusion. The definitional emphasis of financial inclusion varies across countries and geographies, depending on the level of social, economic and financial development and priorities of social concerns. Broadly, financial inclusion means access to finance and financial services for all in a fair, transparent and equitable manner at an affordable cost. It refers to a process that ensures access, availability and usage of the financial system for all, inclusive in terms of people, area and sectors. Theoretically, this definition assumes efficient market hypothesis based on perfect competition. In a perfect competitive financial market, there are no frictions. It is financially inclusive and facilitates efficient allocation of financial resources and welfare by providing a whole range of efficient financial services. Hence, there is no problem of financial exclusion in an inclusive perfect financial system.

The perfect inclusive financial market system, though theoretically sound, however does not exist. Financial markets are not perfect due to asymmetric information and distortions in terms of availability, accessibility and affordability to all members of the economy. Economic stratification is inevitable in imperfect market. It integrates some and marginalises others. Market exclusion is, therefore, inherent in imperfect market. As a result, access to financial services is restricted and financial market exclusion takes place in terms of people, area and sectors. The research work on asymmetric information and principal agent theory led by Nobel laureates Joseph Stiglitz and George Akerlof have made economists and policymakers to think about the imperfections in financial markets and the central role of financial intermediaries in economic development.

In the context of financial market imperfections, financial inclusion is defined in terms of financial exclusion from the financial system. Financial exclusion implies existence of obstacles to the use of financial products and services. Hence, it is defined in terms of financial exclusion as inability to access necessary financial services in an appropriate form due to financial market imperfections. Over the years, several definitions of financial inclusion/exclusion have evolved and are shown in Box 2.1.

The definition of financial inclusion in terms of financial exclusion, though a restrictive one, focuses on people excluded and more so poor people without money or assets. It is construed as the inability to access necessary financial services in an appropriate form due to problems associated with access, conditions, prices, marketing or self-exclusion in response to discouraging experiences or perceptions of individuals/entities.

It also refers to the processes that serve to prevent certain social groups and individuals from gaining access to the existing financial system. Since the policymakers are more interested in reaching the unreached, access to finance by the poor and vulnerable groups is considered a prerequisite for empowerment, employment, economic growth, poverty reduction and social cohesion. In the context of policy paradigm of inclusive growth, financial inclusion has become a policy priority in many countries.

Recognising the critical importance of financial inclusion for inclusive economic development in India, the Rangarajan Committee on Financial Inclusion defines financial inclusion as the process of ensuring access to financial services and timely and adequate credit where needed by vulnerable groups such as the weaker sections and low-income groups at an affordable cost (Government of India, 2008a). Thus, financial inclusion, in the Indian context, implies the provision of affordable financial services *viz.*, access to payments and remittance facilities, savings, loans and insurance services by the formal financial system to those who tend to be excluded (RBI, 2008). It may include a basic no-frills banking account for making and receiving payments, savings products suited to the pattern of cash flows of a poor household, money transfer facilities, small loans and overdrafts for productive, personal and other purposes. The emphasis is, thus placed on affordability of these financial services, ability to understand them and access the financial services without any obstacles. However, inclusive finance does not require that every one who is eligible uses these

Box 2.1

Definitions of Financial Inclusion/Exclusion

Sources/Author	*Definition*
ADB (2000)	Provision of a broad range of financial services such as deposits, loans, payment services, money transfers and insurance to poor and low-income households and their microenterprises.
Stephen P. Sinclair (2001)	Financial exclusion means the inability to access necessary financial services in an appropriate form. Exclusion can come about as a result of problems with access, conditions, prices, marketing or self-exclusion in response to negative experiences or perceptions.
Chant Link and Associates (2004)	Financial exclusion is lack of access by certain consumers to appropriate low cost, fair and safe financial products and services from main stream providers. Financial exclusion becomes a concern in the community when it applies to lower income consumers and/or those in financial hardship.
Treasury Committee, House of Commons, UK (2004)	Ability of individuals to access appropriate financial products and services.
Scottish Government (2005)	Access for individuals to appropriate financial products and services. This includes having the capacity, skills, knowledge and understanding to make the best use of those products and services. Financial exclusion by contrast is the converse of this.
United Nations (2006)	A financial sector that provides 'access' to credit for all 'bankable' people and firms, to insurance for all insurable people and firms and to savings and payment services to every one. Inclusive finance does not require that everyone who is eligible use each of the services, but they should be able to choose to use them if desired.
Rangarajan Committee on Financial Inclusion (2008a)	The process of ensuring access to financial services and timely and adequate credit where needed by vulnerable groups such as weaker sections and low income groups at an affordable cost.
World Bank (2008)	Broad access to financial services implies an absence of price and non-price barriers in the use of financial services; it is difficult to define and measure because access has many dimensions.

Source: Compiled by RBI in Chapter VII, "Financial Inclusion", *Report on Currency and Finance.* 2003-08 V: 297.

services, but they should be able to choose to use them, if they so desired (Government of India, 2008).

Inclusive Growth and Financial Inclusion

Inclusive growth and financial inclusion—which comes first, is a million dollar question. The earlier theories of development have focused on accelerating growth and concentrated on capital as a critical factor for growth. Finance was never considered as a factor for growth. The growth was considered as a precondition for the financial sector development. The rise in income inequality was an inevitable consequence of the early stages of development. Trickle-down theory would take care of the inequality. The emphasis was on the need to develop a vibrant and extensive financial system that could tap savings and then channel the funds so generated to a wide spectrum of developmental activities. The main assumption behind these theories was the assumption of perfect competition and efficient market allocation of capital. The public policy focused on redistribution of wealth.

There is now genuine and wide-spread recognition about the adverse social consequences of accelerated growth, which do not seem to be mitigated through the "trickle-down" mechanism. The recent theories of development advocate inclusive growth, which is defined as a "Growth process which yields broad based benefits and ensures equality of opportunity for all" (GoI, 2008b). Growth does not benefit all. The benefits of growth tend to concentrate in the hands of those who have access to the financial system. Inclusive growth encompasses ideas related to basic needs and equity. It focuses on broad-based growth so that growth covers all strata of society. It seeks to bridge the various divides that may fragment the society. Reduction in poverty and disparities of income and ensuring every one a basic minimum standard of living are the objectives of inclusive growth. In this context, access to finance by the poor and vulnerable groups has to be recognised as a pre-requisite for poverty reduction and social cohesion. It has to become an integral part of the efforts to promote inclusive growth (Rangarajan, 2008).

A large body of empirical research also shows that financial market imperfections limit the access to finance to few and thereby, perpetuate income inequalities. Developing inclusive financial system and improving access to finance may accelerate economic growth along with a reduction in income inequality and poverty. Without an inclusive financial system, poor individuals, small enterprises and poor areas have to rely on their own limited savings and earnings to invest in their education and entrepreneurship to take advantages of growth opportunities (World Bank, 2008).

Finance is, therefore, considered critical for inclusive growth. The lack of access to finance is an important factor responsible for persistent income inequality as well as slower growth. Inclusive growth cannot be achieved without financial inclusion. Access to safe, easy and affordable credit and other financial services by the poor and vulnerable groups, disadvantaged areas and lagging sectors is, therefore recognised as a pre-condition for accelerating growth and reducing income disparities and poverty. An inclusive financial system creates equal opportunities to enable economically and socially excluded people to integrate better into the economy and actively contribute to development.

Broadly, the growth benefits of financial inclusion can be conceived from three angles, which are inter-related. First, from the angle of individuals/families, access to a well-functioning financial system can economically and socially empower individuals/families particularly belonging to poor section of the society. It enables them to seize growth opportunities to improve their economic status and thereby integrate into the economy, actively contribute to the development and also protect themselves against economic shocks. Second, from the angle of small and medium firms, access to finance can promote new-firm entry, enterprise growth, innovation, and diversification and risk reduction. Third, from the societal/national perspective, financial inclusion may lead to increase in aggregate output or welfare by realising the growth potential of the bottom of the pyramid.[2]

Financial exclusion, on the other hand, leads to social exclusion, poverty as well as all other associated economic and social problems. According to the Treasury Committee, UK (2006), financial exclusion can impose significant costs on individuals, families and society as a

---

2. Dr. Vijay Kelkar, Chairman of Finance Commission in N.P. Sen Memorial Lecture at Hyderabad (2008) considered financial inclusion as a quasi public good as it is as important as access to safe water or primary education.

whole. They include: (i) barriers to employment as employers may require wages to be paid into a bank account, (ii) opportunities to save and borrow can be difficult to access, (iii) owning or obtaining assets can be difficult, (iv) difficult in smoothening income to cope with shocks, and (v) exclusion from mainstream society.

In 2000, the United Nations adopted the Millennium Development Goals (MDGs), which include inter alia eradicating poverty in all its forms by 2015, universal primary education, gender equality and health related indicators (reduction in child and maternal mortality, and reversing the spread of AIDS, malaria and other diseases). While financial inclusion is not explicitly mentioned among these goals, but it is well recognised that financial inclusion is an important direct or indirect contributor to the achievement of most of the goals. Better access to financial services improves incomes and therefore, the possibility of obtaining better health and education services. Allowing women direct access to financial services will improve their possibilities to become entrepreneurs, thus increasing their incomes, their chances to become more independent and their participation in family and community decision-making. There is also insurance effect: better access to credit, savings and insurance services provide a buffer against income and health shocks. The goal of global cooperation will be hard to attain without better functioning of global financial markets. Thus, the link between financial inclusion and the MDGs is obvious and critical.

Improving access and building inclusive financial systems is, thus, a goal that is relevant to economies at all levels of development. In India, inclusive growth or equitable growth has been the central objective right from the inception of the planning process. Despite higher growth in recent years, a significant proportion of the population in both rural and urban areas could not take advantage of growth opportunities. There is also growing concern arising from an inadequate reduction in poverty levels, sectoral divergences in growth and employment opportunities and tardy improvement in other social indicators. The Eleventh Five Year Plan, therefore, re-emphasised the need for a more inclusive growth. Inclusive financial system creates enabling conditions to bring large number of people, potential entrepreneurs, small enterprises and others who have immense potential to play a critical role in achieving the objective of faster and more inclusive growth.

Financial Exclusion Dimensions

The definitional emphasis on financial exclusion has three dimensions such as 'breadth', 'focus' and 'degree' of exclusion. The breadth dimension links financial exclusion to social exclusion, which defines financial exclusion as the processes that prevent poor and disadvantaged social groups from gaining access to the financial system (Leyshon and Thrift, 1995). It is measured in terms of people excluded. In an under-developed financial system, certain segments of the population experience difficulties in obtaining appropriate access to financial services. The focus dimension links financial exclusion to potential difficulties faced by excluded segments in accessing financial system (Meadows *et al.*, 2004). It is assessed in terms of access barriers such as price, terms and conditions, appropriateness of products etc. It also includes various segments of excluded population such as individuals, households, communities etc. The focus dimension varies depending on the socioeconomic characteristics of the various excluded segments of the community. The degree dimension, on the other hand, links exclusion from particular financial products or services such as credit, insurance, bill-payment services etc. (Rogaly, 1999).

There is also the question of financial exclusion in terms of area or region, sectors and institutions. Financial inclusion refers to access to formal financial institutions such as banks, insurance companies and microfinance institutions. Informal providers of financial services are excluded. Similarly, the backward or undeveloped regions are usually neglected by formal institutions and excluded from financial inclusion. Similarly, agriculture, small and microenterprises and informal service sectors are often neglected by the financial sector. This is also true for the sporadic financing requirements of low-income households for non-productive consumption purposes and other emergency requirements such as medical expenditure etc. Notwithstanding all these, there is a likelihood of voluntary exclusion. People may have access to financial services, but may not wish to use them because such services are unsuiting their needs.

The nature and forms of financial exclusion thus vary considerably according to the dimensions and within dimension, relative to some standards. Early discussion on financial exclusion focused predominantly on the issue of geographical access to financial services, in particularly banking outlets (Leyshon and Thrift, 1993). However, financial exclusion is not just about physical access. It is broadened to include social exclusion focused on access to particular financial products and services provided by the mainstream financial system. There is also shift in emphasis from physical access to wider dimension covering availability and usage of products and services at affordable prices. From the public policy perspective, they are mostly context-specific originating from country-specific problems of financial exclusion dimensions, public policy concerns and socioeconomic conditions.

In India, the financially excluded sections comprise largely assetless low-income small and marginal farmers, landless labourers, oral lessees, unemployed youth; people engaged in unorganised sector, women, old people, physically challenged people and urban slum dwellers. The financial institutions consider them unbankable because they do not have enough income or too high a lending risk. However, in many developing countries, even non-poor households, micro, small and medium entrepreneurs also have difficulty in accessing financial services. Even amongst those who have access to finance, most are underserved in terms of quality and quantity of products and services and significant proportion depends on services of unsustainable poorly performing institutions. The contractual and informational framework might prevent financial institutions from reaching out to this section of community because the outreach is too costly to be commercially viable. There is also difference between access to and use of financial services. There are people who have access but do not use financial services for cultural or religious reasons or because they do not see any need. These non-users include households who prefer to deal in cash depending on their own resources.

Factors Affecting Financial Exclusion

The factors responsible for financial exclusion are varied and thus, no single factor could explain the phenomenon. Broadly, they can be classified as demand-side factors and supply-side factors. The supply-side factors mainly emanate from the structural operation of financial service providers. The principal barriers in the exclusion of financial services are physical access, high charges, penalties and conditions attached to financial products, which make them inappropriate or complicated and perceptions of financial service institutions which are thought to be unwelcoming to low-income people (Sinclair, 2001). The physical access is mainly due to absence of network of the financial service providers, resulting lack of access in terms of distance. Large urban neighbourhoods and densely populated areas have more physical access, while rural population generally have harder time accessing financial services. Remote areas are the most poorly served. The availability of communication, transport and other infrastructure facilities are also important in determining the easy physical access to financial services.

Other important supply-side barriers are convenience of the branch time, appropriateness of products and services, cumbersome procedure/documents required, collateral requirements, language, staff attitude, high charges and penalties, costs and risk perception of financial institutions about the poor. There are many reasons why formal financial institutions do not offer low-income and poor customers more access to financial services. The poor and low-income people have latent demand, but that cannot be satisfied by the financial products or terms and conditions and delivery practices offered by the financial institutions. Their requirements are practical, convenient, affordable, flexible, continuously available, reliable and safe financial services (UN, 2006). The formal financial institutions often do not "look through the eyes of their customers".

The demand-side factors mainly emanate from socioeconomic conditions of financial service users. They include mainly lack of awareness, assetlessness resulting difficulty in offering collateral required, low income and low productivity leading to weak and non-viable demand, lower social status resulting in social exclusion and financial illiteracy barriers and information asymmetry. The most conspicuous demand-side barriers are low income and assetlessness. Financial status of people is always important in gaining access to financial services. Access to credit is frequently limited for women who do not have or cannot hold title to assets such as land and property or must seek male guarantees to borrow. Other factors affecting access to financial services to some extent are: gender issues (access to credit for women limited), age factor (senior citizens and young are usually discriminated), legal hurdles (non-availability of appropriate legal rights documents and psychological and cultural barriers resulting in self-exclusion.

Based on the factors contributing, various forms of financial exclusion are identified (RBI, 2008). They are:

- Access exclusion—restriction of access both physical and financial emanating from the structural operation of financial system.

- Condition exclusion—terms and conditions attached to financial products and services which make them inappropriate for the needs of some segments of population.

- Price exclusion—prices charged are not affordable.

- Marketing exclusion—market excludes some section of the population if they do not have entitlement.

- Self-exclusion—people voluntarily decide not to opt for a financial product because of the fear of refusal to access by the service providers.

The empirical studies carried out in different countries identified a number of factors affecting access to financial products and services. They are summarised in Box 2.2.

Financial Inclusion Strategies in Different Countries

The problem of financial exclusion is a global phenomenon. Globally, over two billion population are found excluded from access to financial services. In a landmark research work titled "Building Inclusive Financial Sectors for Development", the UN had raised the basic question: "why are so many bankable people unbanked?" (UN, 2006).

Box 2.2

Factors Affecting Access to Financial Services

- **Gender issues**: Access to credit is often limited for women who do not have, or cannot hold title to assets such as land and property or must seek male guarantees to borrow.

- **Age factor**: Financial service providers usually target the middle of the economically active population, often overlooking the design of appropriate products for older and younger potential customers.

- **Legal identity**: Lack of legal identities like identity cards, birth certificates or written records often exclude women, ethnic minorities, economic and political refugees and migrant workers from accessing financial services.

- **Limited literacy**: Limited literacy, particularly financial literacy i.e., basic accounting, business finance skills as well as lack of understanding often constrain demand or financial services.

- **Place of living**: Although effective distance is as much about transportation infrastructure as physical distance factors like density of population, rural and remote areas, mobility of the population (i.e., highly mobile people with no fixed or formal address), insurgency in a location etc., also affect access to financial services.

- **Psychological and cultural barriers**: The feeling that banks are not interested to look into their cause has led to self-exclusion for many of the low-income groups. In some countries, cultural and religious barriers to banking also have been observed.

- **Social security payments**: In those countries where the social security payment systems are not linked to the banking system, banking exclusion has been higher.

- **Bank charges**: High and a range of bank charges have a disproportionate effect on people with low income.

- **Terms and conditions**: Terms and conditions attached to products such as minimum balance requirements, and conditions relating to the use of accounts often dissuade people from using such products/services.

- **Level of income**: Financial status of people is always important in gaining access to financial services. Extremely poor people find it difficult to access financial services even when the services are tailored for them. Perception barriers and income discrimination among potential members/in group-lending programmes may exclude the poorer members of the community.

- **Type of occupation**: Many banks have not developed the capacity to evaluate loan applications of small borrowers and unorganised enterprises and hence tend to deny such loan requests.

- **Attractiveness of the products**: Appropriateness of the financial products/services and how their availability is marketed are crucial in financial inclusion.

Source: Compiled from World Bank, 2008; Asian Development Bank, 2007 and RBI, 2008.

In most developing countries, financial services are only available to a minority of the population. The financially excluded outnumber the financially included. The situation is worse in the least developed countries particularly Sub-Saharan African countries, where more than 80 per cent of the population is excluded from access to formal financial system. The problem of financial exclusion is also found even in several developed countries to the extent of 10 to 20 per cent of the population. "Financial inclusion, thus, has become an issue of worldwide concern, relevant equally in economies of the under-developed, developing and developed nations. Building an inclusive financial sector has gained growing global recognition bringing to the fore the need for development strategies that touch all lives, instead of a selected few" (UN, 2006).

Tom Easton (2005) in a study using the World Bank data relating to 54 countries (excluding India), has shown a positive correlation between the GDP per capita and the financial inclusion in terms of the percentage of households having bank accounts. Bangladesh has the lowest percentage of households having access to banks less than 5 per cent. Thailand and Malaysia, though not very rich in terms of per capita GDP, have higher ratios of 49 per cent and 60 per cent banking penetration respectively. Singapore, the city-state has the distinction of having almost 100 per cent access to banking facilities. In Brazil, it is less than 30 per cent and Russia has it less than 20 per cent.

Historically, the problem of financial exclusion was tackled mainly on supply side in different countries. Broadly, governments in different countries intervened in two ways:

- Through state-driven intervention by way of enacting appropriate statutory instruments.

- Through voluntary effort by the banking institutions to provide affordable banking services to all without discrimination.

The measures undertaken include nationalisation of private banks, promoting specialised banks including national savings banks, concessional lending to low-income groups, enactment of legislations defining the right of access to formal banking services and promoting community-based savings and credit societies and mutual saving banks. Most Asian and African countries resorted to nationalisation of private banks to expand banking services to the excluded and established specialised state-owned banks to serve low-income segments. The strategies adopted included *inter alia* expansion of branch networks and promotion of microfinance institutions and self-help groups. In Bangladesh, the establishment of Grameen Bank played the lead role in pushing the frontier of finance for the poor.

The developed countries have also initiated specific measures to bring financially excluded people within the fold of the financial system. The measures adopted, among others, include legislation-backed norms, voluntary code of practices, basic bank accounts and subsidised accounts for the low-income groups.[3] In UK, one out of 12 households does not have bank account with any bank. A Treasury Committee on financial inclusion set up in 2006, identified three priority areas for the purpose of financial inclusion, namely, access to banking services, access to affordable credit and access to free face-to-face money advice.

Among the initiatives taken to promote financial inclusion include:

1. Establishment of financial inclusion fund of UK pound 120 million to support initiatives to tackle financial exclusion.

2. Set up a fund of UK pound 45 million for free face-to-face money advice targeted in areas of high financial exclusion. The fund is administered by the Department of Trade and Industry (DTI) and the face-to-face advice is provided by citizen's advice bureau, community development groups etc.

3. Assignment of responsibility to banks and credit unions to remove financial exclusion.

4. Introduction of 'no-frills' basic bank account and 24 hours basic banking services.

5. Creation of post office current account for those unable or unwilling to access a basic bank account.

6. Introduction of a 'savings gateway' for those on low-income employment. Under this arrangement, for every UK pound saved by those on low-income employment, the state will contribute an

---

3. Country-experiences in financial inclusion are compiled from various sources including Rangarajan Committee Report. For references, see Bibliography.

equivalent UK pound subject to limit upto UK pound 25 per month.

7. Setting up of community finance learning initiatives to promote basic financial literacy among housing association tenants and other disadvantaged groups.

In the USA, about 20 per cent of households lack a bank account. Among the low-income families earning less than US $25000 per annum, around 22 per cent do not have a current or saving bank account. The US government has taken a number of initiatives to bring the financially excluded into financial inclusion. Community Re-investment Act (CRA) enacted for this purpose prohibits discrimination by banks against families with low and moderate incomes. All the licensed and chartered banks have been mandated to fulfil social obligations by enabling access to banking services to excluded sections. Under this Act, the Federal Bank regulatory agencies rate banks on their efforts and effectiveness at serving low-income communities.

Other initiatives undertaken in USA include no minimum balance requirement, low fees, universal saving accounts, saving by the poor matched by the government, free ATM facility and one-time subsidy of US $12.60 for every account opened by the poor. Mortgage lending to people living in deprived parts of the country is also used as a key instrument of financial inclusion. It is also interesting to note that in the US, the Department of Treasury established in 2002 an Office of Financial Education. This office coordinates the financial education efforts of banks and other bodies and promotes access to financial education tools and effective education practices for financial inclusion.

France was in the forefront in promotion of financial inclusion. The Banking Act of 1984 made access to a bank account a legal right. Accordingly, any person of French nationality has the right to open an account with any bank in France. If refused, the aggrieved person can approach the Bank of France, its central bank. On receipt of complaint, the Bank of France will identify and nominate an institute to provide the bank account to the complainant. In 1992, banks in France signed a charter committing themselves to opening bank accounts at an affordable cost with related payment facilities to all. In Germany, the banking industry has adopted voluntarily 'current accounts for everyone' to provide current accounts on demand.

In Canada, a legislation entitled "Access to Basic Banking Services Regulations" was enacted in 2003, to ensure that all Canadians could open personal bank accounts and encash most government cheques at no charge. The Federal Government has also legislation, requiring banks to offer a standard low-cost bank account with a basket of services to low-income groups. Memorandum of Understanding (MoU) were also signed between the Federal Government and banks/financial institutions to ensure that all Canadians have access to affordable banking services.

In Africa, the UNDP with the help of United Nations Capital Development Fund (UNCDF) initiated a regional programme called BISFA (Building Inclusive Financial Sector in Africa) for financial inclusion in African countries in 2004. Its goal is to contribute to the achievement of the MDGs particularly the specific goal of reducing poverty by half by 2015 through increasing sustainable access to financial services in Sub-Saharan Africa for poor and low-income people and for micro and small enterprises. The programme follows three-step process for financial inclusion: (i) conducting a financial sector assessment in each country, (ii) working through an open, participatory process with multiple stakeholders to develop policy, strategy and a national policy for building an inclusive financial sector, and (iii) assisting policymakers and a broad range of financial institutions, development agencies, the private sector and other financial market participants to implement this action plan.

South Africa launched in 2004 "Mzansi", a low-cost national bank account for extending banking services to low-income market segments for which the banking services were elusive till recently. It is a card based saving account with easy availability at accessible outlets like merchant point-of-sale and post offices. This initiative has put access to banking services within the proximity of 15 km for all citizens. Even an ATM service is made available within 10 km of their homes. By end of August 2005, more than 1.5 million Mzansi accounts were opened by people who had never availed banking facilities before.

Some countries like Bolivia, Indonesia and Bangladesh adopted microfinance institutions to provide poor and low-income segments of the society access to financial services and thereby promote financial inclusion. In Mexico, there are around 500 savings and credit societies to provide financial services to low- and medium-income families.

All these clearly show that in both developing and developed countries, the financial inclusion was recognised as an important instrument for socioeconomic development of the poor and disadvantaged groups. As banking services are considered as quasi-public good, it is essential that availability of banking services to the entire population without discrimination should constitute one of the prime objectives of the banking policy. To this end, strategies for building inclusive financial system have to be creative, flexible and appropriate to the national situation. Various proactive and positive actions have been initiated in this direction by the governments in different countries worldwide, which can be used to draw lessons for policy formulation on financial inclusion in the Indian context.

It may be expedient to remember that even in the developed countries having advanced banking facilities, hundred per cent financial inclusion has not been achieved in the real sense of the term. This, however, should not deter us from planning for achieving total financial inclusion, adopting programmes compatible with the diversities prevalent in the Indian situation.

3   An Assessment of Financial Exclusion in India

In India, the widening of access to financial services has been considered, though not explicitly, as one of the objectives of financial sector policies since Independence. After nationalisation of major banks in 1969, the banking policies were, in fact, shaped by the continuous concern regarding a large segment of low-income population left out of the fold of the formal financial system especially in rural areas. The critical issue in the context of financial inclusion is to assess how inclusive Indian financial system is and what is the nature and extent of financial exclusion. A comprehensive assessment of financial inclusion/exclusion in the Indian context, therefore, needs hardly any emphasis.

No comprehensive data are, however, available to analyse the various dimensions of financial inclusion/exclusion in India. An assessment of financial inclusion/exclusion in Indian context has to be, therefore, made based on whatever partial information available from various sources such as 2001 Census, National Sample Surveys, All India Debt and Investment Survey and various banking data published by RBI from time to time. In this chapter, an attempt is made to empirically assess and determine the extent or degree of financial inclusion/exclusion in India and their dimensional characteristics from various perspectives based on whatever secondary data available.

Measures of Financial Inclusion/Exclusion

While there is some element of clarity on conceptual framework of financial inclusion/exclusion, as adumbrated in the earlier chapter, the literature on the subject lacks a common approach that can be used to assess the degree or extent of financial inclusion/exclusion. While the standard indicators of financial depth and efficiency such as the deposit and lending structure of the banking system, capital markets and insurance sector in terms of outreach and deployment of resources are widely available, they do not provide information about the degree or extent of financial inclusion and who has access to which financial products and services. Aggregate data on these indicators can be misleading. For instance, the total number of bank accounts far exceeds the number of customer-households served as households and enterprises have business with several banks or multiple accounts with a single bank. They do not show how many households are excluded. There is, thus, at present no universally accepted single measure for assessing and determining financial inclusion or exclusion.

Theoretically, it is difficult to measure financial inclusion because access has many dimensions. Moreover, access is conceptually different from use of financial services. Financial services include a range of financial products and services. The partial indicators such as population per bank branch or number of saving or credit accounts for a given population, proportion of households indebted, etc., are usually used as indicators to measure financial inclusion/exclusion. They, however, provide only partial information on the level of financial inclusion in an economy. They do not show clearly the extent and magnitude of the financial inclusion/exclusion for a range of financial products and services. They can be considered, at the most, as proxies for financial inclusion/exclusion for basic financial services.

Multiple indicators such as proportion of population of different category, who uses the services of any formal financial institutions, proportion of different category of population with different types of bank accounts, category of people receiving money regularly through formal financial instruments, people keeping money in formal financial institutions, and people who have obtained credit facilities from formal financial institutions are important to assess the nature and extent of financial inclusion/exclusion. However, this requires census data or household surveys on the number and characteristics of households that have availed different type of financial services from different type of financial institutions.[1] There is, thus, a need for accurate comprehensive financial inclusion/exclusion measure which would take into consideration a holistic set of financial products and services, usage by whom and in what quantities and at what price and terms, and characteristics of the households, who are financially included/excluded.

Bank Network Outreach

One of the indicators for measuring banking access is the population per branch. It reflects physical access to banking. Without a bank branch nearby and easily accessible, financial inclusion cannot take place and such areas are financially excluded. In India, the branch network of commercial banks expanded rapidly after nationalisation of 14 major commercial banks in 1969. It has increased from 8262 bank branches in 1969 to 70018 bank branches in 2007. The rural bank branches as a percentage of total bank branches have increased from 22 per cent in 1969 to 41 per cent in 2007. The country has at present 32459 bank branch network in rural areas. As a result, population per bank branch declined from 63000 per bank branch in 1969 to 16000 per bank branch in 2008 (Table 3.1). In rural areas, it has declined from 82000 per bank branch in 1969 to 17000 per bank branch in 2007 showing financial deepening in rural India.

The population-bank intensity across states has shown signs of improving in the recent years. It varies from 12000 in southern states to 22000 in north-eastern states. Notwithstanding the wider geographical coverage by bank branches, at present only 5.2 per cent of the villages are having bank branches and most of the branches are situated at semi-urban areas.

However, India has a network of over 1,00,000 cooperatives throughout the country. With the total credit outlets of 1,59,912 (including banking), the country has, on an average, one credit outlet for

---

1. In India, though for the first time, the decadal census collects information on households availing banking services, it is not comprehensive enough to measure accurately financial inclusion/exclusion. NSSO conducts household indebtedness survey periodically. Though these surveys provide useful information on indebtedness, they do not cover other financial products and services. There is a need for conducting separate household surveys relating to various dimension of financial inclusion/exclusion.

around 5000 population or using a family factor of 5, one credit outlay for every 1000 rural households. This shows that in India, financial inclusion in terms of institutional network outreach is not very poor.

Table 3.1

Financial Inclusion: Outreach

(Population per bank branch)

Year (End March)	Rural	Urban	All Branch Average
1969	82000	33000	63000
1981	20000	17000	19000
1991	14000	16000	14000
2007	17000	13000	16000

Source: Basic Statistical Returns of Scheduled Commercial Banks in India, RBI.

Access to Financial Services

Though the population per bank branch is one of the indicators for measuring physical access to banking, it does not disclose the nature and dimension of financial exclusion. Despite an impressive branch network throughout India, the banking penetration at the household level remains at a low level of 35.5 per cent according to the 2001 Census data.

Table 3.2

Households Availing Banking Services

	Households (in Lakh)	Percentage
Rural	416.40	30.11
Urban	265.90	49.52
Total	682.30	35.54

Source: Census of India—2001, H-Series.

Only 682.30 lakh households out of 1919.64 lakh households were reported to have availed banking services. In the rural areas, the banking outreach is still lower. Out of 1382.72 lakh rural households, only 416.40 lakh households (30 per cent) have access to banking services. In urban areas, on the other hand, 49.5 per cent of the urban households have availed banking facilities. Over 12 crore households in India, of whom more than 9 crore in rural India are yet to be touched by banking sector. These findings are more or less confirmed by NCAER survey in 2008, which indicated that at the end of June 2005, 23.9 per cent of all households had loan outstanding; 20.9 per cent in urban and 25.2 per cent in rural areas.

Institutional (banks and cooperative societies) and non-institutional (moneylenders, landlords, relatives and friends) sources are broadly the main sources of supply of financial products and services for households. Prior to Independence, institutional sources played hardly any role in providing financial services to households particularly in rural areas. Non-institutional sources were the main source of financial services. In 1971, the percentage of the number of households indebted to institutional sources in rural areas was only 24 and the remaining 76 per cent households relied for their financial needs on non-institutional sources (Table 3.3).

Table 3.3

Financial Inclusion: Institutional and Non-Institutional Sources

(Percentage of indebted households)

Agency	Rural				Urban			All		
	1971	1981	1991	2002	1981	1991	2002	1981	1991	2002
Institutional	24.0	48.8	66.7	50.6	46.0	61.1	52.2	48.2	65.4	50.9
Non-institutional	76.00	51.2	41.9	58.5	54.0	48.7	52.8	51.8	43.4	57.3
All agencies	100.0	100.0	100.0	100.0	100.0	100.0	100.0	100.0	100.0	100.0

Source: All India Debt and Investment Survey, various rounds, RBI.

After the nationalisation of banks, the share of number of households indebted to institutional sources increased sharply, while that of indebted to non-institutional sources declined correspondingly. However in recent years, trend is reversed; the shares of households indebted to institutional sources in the total indebted households declined, while the households indebted to non-institutional sources increased. The decline was relatively more significant among rural households. This has serious implications for financial inclusion in India.

Credit account penetration (credit accounts per 100 persons) is another important though partial indicator of the financial inclusion/exclusion. Analysis of credit accounts per 100 persons/adults in Table 3.4 presents a very dismal picture of expansion of credit delivery services in India despite significant increase in the bank branch networks.

Table 3.4

Credit and Deposit Accounts with Commercial Banks: March 2007

(Number)

Areas	Indicators of Coverage	Credit Accounts	Deposit Accounts
Rural	Accounts per 100 persons	6.5	26.2
	Accounts per 100 adults	9.6	38.8
Urban	Accounts per 100 persons	13.1	50.7
	Accounts per 100 adults	19.5	75.2
Total	Accounts per 100 persons	8.3	33.0
	Accounts per 100 adults	12.4	48.9

Source: Basic Statistical Returns of Scheduled Commercial Banks in India, RBI.

In rural areas, credit accounts per 100 persons work out to only 6.5 and for adults, 9.6. It shows that 90 per cent of the adult population in rural areas has no access to credit services from the commercial banks. Even in urban areas, though the number of credit accounts per 100 persons/adults is more than double, it is still low compared to any developed countries. For both urban and rural areas, credit accounts per 100 persons work out to 8.3 and per 100 adults, 12.4. If the credit accounts of all primary cooperative credit societies and SHGs are included, credit penetration from the institutional sources work out to 17 per 100 persons and 25 per 100 adults. This indicates that 75 per cent of earning adult population remain excluded from the credit facilities from the institutional sources.

Likewise, the facility of deposits is another key instrument of financial inclusion. Access to the facility of depositing promotes thrift and develops the habit of saving. It enables people to plan their future and borrow from the banks for undertaking any income generating activities or for any contingencies. The number of saving accounts per 100 persons is 33 and per 100 adults, 48.9. In rural areas, it is 26.2 per 100 persons and 38.8 per 100 adults, while in urban areas, it is 50.7 and 75.2 respectively. While interpreting the data, it should be noted that multiple deposit accounts are held by many account holders and the data also include the dormant accounts. Notwithstanding this limitation, the number of deposit accounts per population in rural areas provides some insights into the magnitude of financial exclusion in terms of access to saving facilities.[2]

Financial Exclusion by Economic/Social Status

The findings of the NSS 59th Round (2003) reveal that 45.9 million farmer households in the country (51.4 per cent) out of a total 89.35 million farm households do not have access to credit either from institutional or non-institutional sources (Table 3.5). The magnitude of financial exclusion would be higher if all rural households are considered. Out of 149 million rural households, 92 million (62 per cent) are found to be financially excluded.

Table 3.5

Extent of Financial Inclusion/Exclusion by Occupational Groups

Occupational Groups	Households (million)			Percentage	
	Included	*Excluded*	*Total*	*Included*	*Excluded*
Small/marginal farmers	34.70	40.27	74.97	46.29	53.71
Medium/large farmers	8.72	5.66	14.38	60.64	39.36
Total farmers	43.42	45.93	89.35	48.60	51.40
Agricultural labourers	4.50	16.70	21.20	21.20	78.80
Artisans	2.20	5.50	7.70	28.60	71.40
Others	6.20	24.40	30.60	20.30	79.70
Total non-cultivators	13.00	46.60	59.60	21.80	78.20
Total rural households	56.51	92.44	148.95	37.94	62.06

Note: Financial inclusion in the table refers to indebtedness to both formal and Informal agencies.
Source: Situation Assessment Survey, 59th Round NSSO, 2003.

---

2.   The data available from various sources show that at present only 40 per cent of the households have cheque accounts, 10 per cent life insurance, 0.6 per cent non-life insurance, 2 per cent credit cards and 13 per cent ATM-debit cards.

Among farmer households, 54 per cent of marginal and small farmers are found financially excluded. As against this, the financially excluded constitutes only 39 per cent among medium and large farmers. It clearly demonstrates that the ability to access credit increases with the increase in size of farm holdings. The NSS data also shows that 87 per cent of non-indebted farm households (financially excluded) belong to the marginal and small farmer categories. Only 13 per cent belong to medium and large farmer categories.

If the financially excluded are considered as those households not having any access to formal financial institutions only, the picture that emerges is furthermore dismal. Only 27 per cent of total farm households are indebted to formal sources. In other words, out of 89.35 million farm households, 64.95 farm households, which constitute 73 per cent of total farm households, do not have any access to formal credit sources. The majority of the financially included among marginal/small farmer households is indebted to informal sources and remains excluded from the formal financial system.

The incidence of financial exclusion among non-cultivator households is found to be the highest (78 per cent) in rural India. Out of 59.6 million non-cultivator households, about 46.6 million are estimated to be financially excluded. The agricultural labourers, artisans and other non-cultivator families are mostly asset-less resource-poor households in rural areas. The financial exclusion constitutes 78.8 per cent among agricultural labourer households, 71.4 per cent among artisans and 79.7 among other non-cultivator families respectively.

Table 3.6 shows the level of financial exclusion across social groups among farmer households in rural areas. The analysis of data shows that the highest level of financial exclusion is found among scheduled tribes (63.7 per cent). This is apparently due to their living in remote rural/tribal areas, where it is difficult to provide financial services.

Surprisingly, the level of access to credit among the scheduled caste farmers is comparable to other social categories of farmers. It is 49.7 per cent among scheduled castes, 48.5 per cent among other backward classes and 50.7 per cent among others. However, it should be noted that most of the scheduled tribe and scheduled caste farm households rely on the non-institutional sources for their credit requirements.

Table 3.6

Financial Inclusion/Exclusion by Social Classes among Farmer Households

Social Class	Households (Lakh)			Percentage	
	Included	Excluded	Total	Included	Excluded
SC farmers	78.3	77.6	155.9	50.23	49.77
ST farmers	43.3	75.9	119.2	36.32	63.68
Other backward classes	191.5	180.0	371.5	51.42	48.58
Others	122.0	124.9	246.9	49.42	50.58
Total	435.1	458.4	893.5	48.64	51.36

Source: 59th Round, NSSO. Credit access include both institutional and non-institutional sources.

Invest India Incomes and Savings Survey conducted by IIMS in 2007 provides the details of the sources of credit facilities availed by different income groups. The details are presented in Table 3.7. The analysis of this data reveals that higher income groups rely increasingly more on institutional sources for financial services and less on non-institutional sources. The recourse to non-institutional sources is relatively higher among lower income groups.

Table 3.7

Sources of Borrowings by Income Groups

(Percentage of indebted earners)

Income Group (Rs. '000)	Institutional Sources	Non-Institutional Sources
Less than 50	27.50	72.50
50–100	46.00	54.00
100–200	59.40	40.60
200–400	60.20	39.80
400 and above	70.50	29.50
All	32.80	67.20

Source: Investment India Market Solutions (IIMS) Survey, 2007.

About 70 per cent of the earners in the annual income bracket of more than Rs.4,00,000 have borrowed from institutional sources as compared to only 27.5 per cent in the case of earners in the income bracket of less than Rs.50,000. About 73 per cent of the earners below the income level of Rs.50000 depend on informal sources for their financial needs.

These findings are also corroborated by the NSS data on asset holdings classes in rural and urban areas. The analysis of NSS data in Table 3.8 shows that the level of financial inclusion is directly linked to income levels represented by asset holding classes.

Table 3.8

Financial Inclusion: Asset Holding-wise (June 2002)

(Per cent of households indebted out of total households)

Asset Holding (Rs. '000)	Rural	Urban
Less than 15	15.00	10.70
15–30	19.00	14.80
30–60	25.20	14.80
60–100	26.50	18.30
100–150	28.90	19.70
150–200	28.70	20.00
200–300	28.70	19.90
300–450	28.70	18.70
450–800	31.00	22.50
800 and above	32.90	21.40
All	26.50	17.80

Source: 59th Round Surveys, NSSO.

In both urban and rural areas, the level of financial inclusion is higher among higher asset groups and vice versa. The higher asset holding households have ability and accessibility to avail financial services by providing collateral. They also possess higher repaying capacity and higher level of confidence of lenders. All these contribute towards their higher access to financial services.

Financial Exclusion: Region-wise

The region-wise analysis of NSS data reveals wide inter-regional disparity in access to financial services. The farm households excluded from accessing credit from formal sources as a proportion to total farm households is as high as 96 per cent in north-eastern, 81 per cent in eastern and 78 per cent in central regions (Table 3.9). These regions taken together account for 64 per cent of the total farm households excluded from accessing credit from formal sources. In southern and western regions, on the other hand, the percentages of financially excluded farm households work out to 57 and 56 respectively.

Table 3.9

Region-wise Extent of Financial Inclusion/Exclusion in Rural Areas

Region	Farm Households (Million)			Percentage Share	
	Total	Included	Excluded	Included	Excluded
Northern	10.95	2.74	8.20	25.05	74.95
North-eastern	3.54	0.14	3.39	4.09	95.91
Eastern	21.06	3.95	17.11	18.74	81.26
Central	27.13	6.08	21.05	22.41	77.59
Western	10.37	4.56	5.81	43.98	56.02
Southern	16.16	6.91	9.25	42.75	57.25
Union territories	0.15	0.02	0.13	10.14	89.86
All-India	89.35	24.40	64.95	27.30	72.70

Note: Financially included/excluded refer to those indebted/non-indebted to formal credit sources and do not include informal sources.

Source: 59th Round, NSSO.

The state-wise NSS data in Table 3.10 indicates that the financial exclusion (proportion of non-indebted farmer households) is most acute in many of the states in the north-eastern, eastern and central regions. It is 68 per cent in Jammu and Kashmir and 67 per cent in Himachal Pradesh in the northern region. In the north-eastern region, almost all states except Tripura have financial exclusion varying between 61 and 96 per cent. In Bihar, it is 67 per cent and Jharkhand, 79 per cent. In the central region, Uttarakhand has the highest financial exclusion (93 per cent), followed by Chhattisgarh (59.8 per cent) and Uttar Pradesh (59.7 per cent).

In the western region, in both Gujarat and Maharashtra, it is slightly less than 50 per cent. More inclusive states are in the southern region. Financial exclusion in these states varies only from 18 per cent in Andhra Pradesh to 38 per cent in Karnataka. In Kerala, it is 36 per cent and in Tamil Nadu, 25 per cent. The financial exclusion is lowest in Andhra Pradesh followed by Tamil Nadu and highest in Meghalaya (96 per cent) followed by Arunachal Pradesh (94 per cent).

Table 3.10

State-wise Extent of Financial Exclusion in Farm Households

State/Region	Non-Indebted Farm Households		State/Region	Non-Indebted Farm Households	
	In lakh	Per cent		In lakh	Per cent
Northern	53.21	48.7	**Eastern**	126.39	60.0
Haryana	9.11	46.9	Bihar	47.42	67.0
Himachal Pradesh	6.03	66.6	Jharkhand	22.34	79.1
Jammu & Kashmir	6.43	68.2	Orissa	22.09	52.2
Punjab	6.38	34.6	West Bengal	34.53	49.9
Rajasthan	25.26	47.6	**Central**	158.29	58.4
North-Eastern	28.36	80.4	Chhattisgarh	16.50	59.8
Arunachal Pradesh	1.15	94.1	Madhya Pradesh	31.09	49.2
Assam	20.51	81.9	Uttar Pradesh	102.38	59.7
Manipur	1.61	75.2	Uttarakhand	8.32	92.8
Meghalaya	2.44	95.9	**Southern**	44.11	27.3
Mizoram	0.60	76.4	Andhra Pradesh	10.84	18.0
Nagaland	0.51	63.5	Karnataka	15.52	38.4
Tripura	1.19	50.8	Kerala	7.82	35.6
Sikkim	0.36	61.2	Tamil Nadu	9.93	25.5
Western	47.92	46.3	UTs	0.99	66.9
Gujarat	18.20	48.1	All-India	459.26	51.4
Maharashtra	29.72	45.2			

Note: Indebted to formal sources only.

Source: 59th Round, NSSO.

The data in Table 3.11 depicts rural-urban divide and inter-regional disparity in both credit and deposit account penetration. In all the regions, credit penetration in urban areas is significantly higher than in rural areas. Except in southern and northern regions, in all other regions, credit account penetration in rural areas is less than 5 accounts per 100 persons.

Table 3.11

*Region-wise Penetration of Credit and Deposit Accounts
of Commercial Banks (March 2007)*

Regions	Credit Accounts (per 1000 persons)			Deposit Accounts (per 100 persons)		
	Rural	*Urban*	*Average of all Branches*	*Rural*	*Urban*	*Average of all Branches*
Northern	5.6	10.0	7.1	29.9	64.1	41.5
North-eastern	4.1	5.5	4.3	18.9	33.6	21.2
Eastern	4.5	6.2	4.8	18.4	44.4	23.3
Central	4.3	5.0	4.4	23.4	40.2	27.4
Western	4.8	18.9	10.5	26.4	53.6	37.5
Southern	14.4	21.6	16.8	38.7	53.8	43.8
All-India	6.5	13.1	8.3	26.2	50.8	33.0

Source: Basic Statistical Returns of Scheduled Commercial Banks in India, RBI.

In northern region, it is 5.6 accounts per 100 persons. In southern region, on the other hand, it is 14.4, almost three times higher. In urban areas, credit penetration is significantly higher in the case of northern, western and southern regions—more than double. It is highest in southern region (21.6), followed by western region (18.9) and Northern region (10.0). It is lowest in central (5.0), followed by north-eastern (5.5) and eastern (6.2).

The region-wise pattern of saving account penetration is in contrast with the region-wise pattern observed in the case of credit account penetration. The inter-regional variations in the spread of deposit accounts are found to be only marginal except in the case of north-eastern and eastern regions. In rural areas, the saving account penetration is highest in southern region (38.7), followed by northern region (29.9), western (26.4) and central (23.4). It is the lowest in the eastern region, followed by north-eastern region (18.9). As against this, in urban areas, northern region has the highest saving account penetration (64.1) followed by southern region (53.8) and western (53.6). The north-eastern region (33.6) has the lowest deposit account penetration, followed by central region (40.2) and eastern (44.4).

To sum up, though India has achieved remarkable progress in institutional network outreach, not much progress is made in financial inclusion. Financial exclusion in terms of access to banking facilities and credit and deposit accounts penetration is still significantly very high. Nearly three-fourths of the households do not have access to formal financial institutions. The magnitude of financial exclusion also varies widely across regions/states, social groups, income levels and asset holdings. The poorer the households are, greater is the financial exclusion. The preponderance of financially excluded population occurs mainly in rural and semi-urban areas. Similarly, more backward regions have higher financial exclusion ratios.

4

Earlier Approaches for Financial Inclusion

India has a long history of banking development. Although the term 'financial inclusion' was not in vogue in India historically, the government and the RBI have undertaken several initiatives over time to tackle the non-availability of banking facilities to the underprivileged and weaker sections of the society. These initiatives include nationalisation of banks, branch expansion through Lead Bank Scheme, prescription of priority sector targets, lending to weaker sections at concessional rates, promotion of microfinance and self-help groups (SHGs) and SHG-bank linkage for microfinance. These initiatives were undertaken at different points in time to expand the outreach of banking facilities and increase the flow of credit to the weaker section of the society.[1] This and the next chapters, therefore, briefly trace the historical and contemporary initiatives undertaken by the Government of India and RBI for financial inclusion.

Evolution of Commercial Banks

Though banking was emerging as an urban-oriented service and accessible to only the rich and educated class, there were exceptions especially in the south, where small banks were serving the persons from the middle class. Banks were promoted by some of the enlightened leaders of the society, who were in the national freedom movement and

---

1. There are three distinct phases in the earlier initiatives. First, the 1950s up to the mid-1960s, cooperatives were considered as the main institutional vehicles for financial services to rural people and weaker section of the society. Second, the 1970s and 1980s, commercial banks and regional rural banks were assigned a major role for financial inclusion. Third, 1990s saw the emergence of SHG movement and growing number of microfinance institutes (MFIs) to fill the institutional space for provision of financial services to the poor and weaker section of the society.

also in the social reform initiatives. Members of the legal profession were in the vanguard in starting schools and banking companies with the resources pooled from the society. However, banking was mostly confined to the business classes and the rich during the last hundred years.

With the dawn of planning era in the fifties, the policymakers slowly started thinking about the need for utilising banks as an instrument of economic development. The All India Rural Credit Survey of 1954, after making a thorough study of the rural credit scenario recommended the nationalisation of Imperial Bank of India with a mandate to open 500 rural branches (RBI, 1956). Imperial Bank of India was functioning with its imperialistic posture, distancing itself away from the common man. State Bank of India came into being in its place in 1955 with some of its new branches operating in rural areas.

Independent India witnessed the proliferation of banking companies in the metropolitan and urban centres, catering to the requirements of big business and industries growing under the Licence Raj. Industrial houses were the promoters and the major beneficiaries of the banking facilities (Thingalaya, 1997). The establishment of National Credit Council under the chairmanship of Prof. D.R. Gadgil paved the way for the introduction of social control on banks in 1968. Some of the important sectors of the economy were recognised as priority sectors and the banks were directed to lend to them on a priority basis (RBI, 1969).

After the nationalisation of banks in 1969, direct lending to small borrowers became an integral part of the lending programmes of banks due to the operational guidelines issued by the Government of India, the owner of banks, and monitored periodically by the Reserve Bank of India. Specific lending programmes like the Differential Interest Rate Scheme and subsidy-linked lending programmes under Integrated Rural Development Programme (IRDP) were introduced. Populist programmes under poverty alleviation schemes also were introduced.

While efforts were made from time to time to extend the reach of the banking sector to the poor, financial inclusion was never considered as a goal to be reached by the banking sector. The broad approach followed in India in 1970s and 1980s was more oriented towards credit requirements of specific sectors and segments of population. There was no emphasis on individual or household level financial inclusion. Since the emergent pattern of economic development itself was also not able to attain inclusive growth even after nearly five decades of planning, inclusive growth for the banking sector did not attract the attention of the policymakers till recently.

Rural Branch Expansion

When banks were nationalised in 1969, there were only 8187 bank branches in India. The ratio of population per branch was very poor. There was one branch for a population of 64000. The number of rural branches was only 1833, constituting 22 per cent of the total branches. Regional inequalities in the availability of banking facilities were very large, depriving a sizeable portion of the population accessibility to banks. One of the first programmes, therefore, introduced was the rapid rural branch expansion programme. The branch licensing policy was made rural branch-oriented, by directing the banks to open four rural branches in order to get a licence for opening one metropolitan or urban branch.

Expansion of rural branches was rightly conceived as a strategy for augmenting rural credit and expanding the rural customer base. Banks in the private sector were concentrating in urban areas for obvious reasons. Public sector banks were compelled to go rural. Barefoot bankers were found in many hitherto unknown villages. After pursuing this goal relentlessly in the 1970s and 1980s, there was a total change in emphasis since the 1990s, when the new generation banks came into being. The latest trend is the emergence of branchless banking, with the tacit support of the regulator.

Public sector banks were under great pressure in the 1970s to open rural branches in the districts allotted to them under the Lead Bank Scheme (LBS). In many cases, in the lead districts, the designated lead banks were having no presence or very little exposure. But they initiated the survey of the districts, identifying unbanked areas for branch opening. The number of rural branches increased to 24,577 during the next 15 years, thanks to the prodding. Perhaps, but for the regimentation of branch expansion, banks would not have opened rural branches in such large numbers.

The tangible result of the branch expansion programme was the dramatic change in the branch distribution pattern of the commercial banks. The share of rural branches has increased from 22 per cent in 1969 to 42 per cent in 2007. However, their share in total banking business remains disproportionately low. Though the rural retail outlets constitute 42 per cent of the branch network, they have single digit shares in both deposit mobilised and credit lent by banks. In deposit mobilisation, their share is 9 per cent and in credit deployment, it is not more than 8 per cent. On the other end are the metropolitan branches, which are less in number but have a lion's share in banking business. These 11,789 branches, forming 16 per cent of the total branch network, mobilise 56 per cent of the total bank deposits. Over 65 per cent of the total credit is lent through them. The concentration of banking business of this magnitude in the metropolitan centres in a large country like ours, certainly calls for a reduction in the regional inequalities. What is more intriguing is the fact that inequalities are more pronounced in terms of the volume of banking business than in terms of the availability of banking outlets.

Along with the expansion in the service points across the states, banks also embarked upon enlarging their customer base through the branches. Opening of savings bank accounts is the first step in initiating the uninitiated. With a small amount of initial deposit, new customers were inducted into the banks. On the branch opening day, invariably hundreds of savings bank passbooks were distributed through the specially invited dignitaries. An amount, as small as Rs.25, was enough to open an account, when the present day procedures of Know Your Customer, insisting on the photo of the depositor were not in vogue. Though many such accounts remained dormant after some time, banks were able to bring to the banking fold many illiterate villagers. There were instances, where the money concealed in pots found their way to the rural branches.

Some interesting data on the expansion of branch network, the increase in the number of savings bank accounts and the number of borrowing accounts during the period 1972 to 2008 are furnished in Table 4.1. The number of branches of banks—the service points, which include administrative offices—has increased from 14,650 in 1972 to 79056 in 2009. Banks have increased their rural presence considerably during the same period. The rural offices constitute 41.5 per cent of the total offices of the banks in India, while the offices in the metropolitan centres account for 17.4 per cent only (RBI, 2008). Geographically, the structure of the Indian banking sector is thus rural-oriented, a fact, which is often not taken note of.

The number of savings bank accounts has gone up from 2.36 crore to 37.35 crore from 1972 to 2007. It may be noted that the number of savings bank accounts is not synonymous with the number of bank customers, as many of the customers in urban areas have more than one savings bank deposit account. An informed estimate of the bank customers derived from the number of savings bank accounts could be about 17 crore at present. The total number of deposit accounts of all types has risen to 52 crore from less than 4 crore after the nationalisation of banks. Interestingly 28.8 per cent of the deposit accounts originate from the rural branches. The share of metropolitan branches is 23.7 per cent. The plausible inference is the preponderance of small deposit accounts in the rural branches.

The spurt in the number of borrowing accounts is equally significant; the increase is from less than a crore to 9.44 crore. The numbers of deposit accounts and borrowing accounts are not additive. Invariably, every borrower would be having a savings bank account.

Taking into consideration of the multiplicity of accounts held by the bank customers, the number of bank customers (not deposit accounts or borrowing accounts) could be estimated at 27 crore. Banks certainly have a long way to go to reach the unreached.

Banks have travelled a long way from their traditional banking environment. The computer-savvy new generation banks have changed the concept of branches as business channels. Brick and mortar branches are substituted by computerised click branches. For improving

Table 4.1

Growth in Service Points and the Number of Customer Accounts

Year	Rural Branches (Number)	Total Branches (Number)	Savings Deposit Accounts (No. crore)	Total Deposit Accounts (No. crore)	Total Borrowing Accounts (No. crore)
1972	5,274	14,650	2.36	3.48	0.43
1973	5,491	15,247	2.59	3.84	0.46
1974	6,069	16,816	3.07	4.54	0.55
1975	6,616	18,575	3.57	5.37	0.62
1976	7,414	20,940	4.19	6.42	0.83
1977	9,122	24,501	5.05	7.85	1.07
1978	11,553	27,979	5.97	9.21	1.30
1979	13,077	30,200	7.01	10.77	1.54
1980	14,818	32,412	8.04	12.39	1.80
1981	17,308	36,037	9.33	14.36	2.07
1982	20,310	40,180	10.27	15.62	2.35
1983	21,981	43,209	11.84	17.75	2.55
1984	24,577	45,747	12.80	19.02	2.95
1985	28,595	52,638	14.56	21.64	3.36
1986	29,733	54,429	16.29	23.72	3.88
1987	30,144	55,150	17.68	25.62	4.34
1988	30,956	56,650	20.07	28.73	4.79
1989	32,840	58,993	21.08	30.20	5.21
1990	34,184	60,515	23.56	33.33	5.38
1991	35,134	61,724	25.30	35.52	6.19
1992	35,254	62,121	26.39	36.97	6.58
1993	35,360	62,774	26.93	37.97	6.21
1994	35,396	63,358	27.65	39.69	5.96
1995	33,017	63,817	27.31	39.00	5.81
1996	32,982	63,026	27.22	39.20	5.66
1997	32,932	63,550	27.14	39.65	5.56
1998	32,878	64,218	27.24	40.00	5.36
1999	32,857	64,939	27.32	40.59	5.23
2000	32,734	65,412	27.43	41.28	5.43
2001	32,562	65,919	28.00	42.80	5.24
2002	32,380	66,190	28.31	43.99	5.64
2003	32,303	66,536	28.92	44.61	5.95
2004	32,121	67,188	30.43	45.71	6.64
2005	32,082	68,355	32.00	46.68	7.71
2006	30,579	69,471	34.34	48.51	8.54
2007	30,551	71,839	37.35	51.92	9.44
2008	31,076	76,050	42.91	58.16	10.70

Source: Basic Statistical Returns of Scheduled Commercial Banks in India, Reserve Bank of India, (various issues).

the accessibility to customers, their reliance is not on the traditional branches. E-banking is being popularised and outsourcing of agents is increasingly being used for reaching out to the growing number of customers. The latest trend is to go for cost effective branchless banking.

Induction of Regional Rural Banks

An institutional innovation made in the field of rural banking, with the avowed objective of reaching out to the rural poor, is the formation of regional rural banks—*gramin* banks.[2] By their constitution, they were designed to operate only in the rural areas, catering to the credit needs of the target groups—the marginal farmers, agricultural labourers, petty traders and families below the poverty line. Though they were thrust upon the rural banking scenario in 1975 by the Government of India driven by its impatience about the slow progress made by banks in rural areas, the new credit agency raised some hopes about its comparative advantages. However, what was conceived as an experimental model to be tried in selected agro-economic zones initially attracted the attention of most of the state governments. Between 1975 and 1987, as many as 196 *gramin* banks came into existence all over the country, excluding Goa, Puducherry, Sikkim and Andaman and Nicobar Islands.

These banks were promoted by the Government of India, the state governments and public sector banks. The ownership of capital was in the ratio of 50:15:35 in each bank. Besides the public sector banks, two private sector banks and a cooperative bank also were designated as the sponsors of these banks. The first bank—*Prathama* Bank—was sponsored by Syndicate Bank in Moradabad in Uttar Pradesh on October 2, 1975.

From the beginning, the manual books of these banks contained many do's and do not's. The manpower constraint was hindering their branch expansion almost since the beginning. The area of operations being limited to a few districts, some of the banks were experiencing limitations to expand. Though conceived as low cost rural credit agencies, the wage revision rendered most of them financially weak. The unremunerative lending programmes made a dent on their bottom lines.

---

2. They were established under the provisions of an ordinance promulgated on the 26th September 1975 and the Regional Rural Bank Act, 1976.

Exceptions, however, were there in plenty, with some of them earning profits comparable with that of some of the private sector banks of the old generation.

Table 4.2

The Growth of Gramin Banks' Outreach

Year	Branches (Number)	Savings Accounts (No. lakh)	Deposit Accounts (No. lakh)	Borrowing Accounts (No. lakh)
1980	2,735	25.37	31.19	n.a.
1981	3,809	36.48	49.12	n.a.
1982	5,455	54.14	67.74	n.a.
1983	6,845	72.00	87.99	n.a.
1984	8,682	87.09	105.65	n.a.
1985	12,176	121.13	145.95	n.a.
1986	12,846	143.54	175.96	n.a.
1987	13,180	170.41	208.08	n.a.
1988	13,673	194.94	238.34	n.a.
1989	14,265	205.81	252.91	n.a.
1990	14,532	243.53	295.92	n.a.
1991	14,697	264.86	32.148	n.a.
1992	14,719	285.49	347.45	n.a.
1993	14,731	297.32	365.22	n.a.
1994	14,727	305.39	377.82	129.88
1995	14,683	312.39	388.81	n.a
1996	14,672	313.71	398.00	130.55
1997	14,639	326.93	423.08	121.02
1998	14,619	343.69	446.40	122.93
1999	14,640	344.33	453.53	111.38
2000	14,639	353.93	474.26	118.58
2001	14,651	366.75	497.05	122.03
2002	14,664	366.89	500.26	126.27
2003	14,671	400.77	536.64	128.73
2004	14,663	428.76	562.85	127.15
2005	14,645	448.69	576.89	141.67
2006	14,607	474.77	597.91	133.94
2007	14,652	526.55	651.09	181.85
2008	14,825	608.88	740.62	161.27

Source: Basic Statistical Returns of Scheduled Commercial Banks in India RBI, (various issues).

Operating mostly in the second-order villages—which are not served by commercial banks—these banks have built up relationship with different strata of the village society. They have been successful in mobilising small savings. They have canvassed 5.26 crore savings bank accounts. Through this process, many of them have been able to raise a substantial proportion of their funds at lower cost. In the case of a few successful *gramin* banks like Gurgaon Gramin Bank, the share of low cost deposits is as high as 66 per cent (Gurgaon Gramin Bank, 2009).

The policymakers' obsession with the propagation of *gramin* banks as low cost rural credit agencies, made them blind to the need for building up an integrated rural credit apparatus from the village level. With a mandate to provide credit to only the target groups, these banks were forced to operate in truncated rural economy, catering to only a section of the rural society. This has adversely affected their viability and growth. Smaller advances to the poorer people, at lower interest rates, operating in smaller premises (with a ceiling on rent) in backward villages, these banks were managed by people drawing lower salaries. Their lending operations were narrowly confined to the target groups— marginal farmers, landless labourers and village artisans. They were not permitted to lend to the borrowers from the non-target groups in their operational areas. Relaxations were made after much damage was done to the viability of the branches. This has led to what may be termed as the underutilisation of the installed capacity of this rural credit agency (Thingalaya, 2002).

The staff members of the *gramin* banks were not provided an exposure to the nuances of managing the credit proposals beyond those of petty small advances. Expertise in handling medium size credit proposals emanating from the rural customers outside the target groups could not be built up during the last 25 years of the existence of these banks in the village set-up. With limited exposure to the outside world and the selections being made locally, the staff was a novice in banking. There was no promotion policy in place for the staff, when these banks started functioning (Thingalaya, 2008). Some banks headed by rural-minded persons could show some good results, while many others just existed in the rural sector.

There were uncertainties about the continuation of these banks, when the financial sector reforms were implemented. However, some of the elements of liberalisation in their operations introduced since then have improved their performance. Relaxation of the restricted lending, partial deregulation of the interest rates and the introduction of a promotion policy for their staff have resulted in strengthening their bottom lines. Some of them have grown stronger than the old generation banks in the private sector, operating under comparable conditions in some states (Thingalaya, 2005). In a comparative study of a *gramin* bank and an old private sector bank, both operating in Kerala, the profit per employee was found to be higher for the *gramin* bank.

After nearly three decades of existence, the policymakers realised the necessity of enlarging the operational areas of *gramin* banks, providing them more space to expand. Based on the recommendations of working groups, which have studied this aspect, they were allowed to extend their branch network to the neighbouring districts on a selective basis. Amalgamation of *gramin* banks sponsored by the same bank at state level was considered as necessary for their development. The process of amalgamation of *gramin* banks introduced recently, though incomplete, is a step in the right direction in revitalising the operational capabilities of these banks. Since September 2005 silently and effectively, 108 *gramin* banks have been amalgamated at the state level, reducing their number from 196 to 86. *Gramin* banks sponsored by the same bank in each state were merged to form bigger banks. Expansion of their operational areas is beneficial to them, as some of them were stagnating, by operating in single districts.

These banks were religiously publishing in their annual reports the number of new deposit and borrowing accounts added during the year. It is regrettable that most of them have stopped publishing these data in the recent years.

Lending to Small Borrowers

For reaching out to the relatively poorer sections of the society, many experiments have been made by the policymakers since bank nationalisation. When the barefoot bankers landed in the rural areas, they were compelled to adopt lending programmes to suit the local population. In the absence of readymade lending programmes, they initially concentrated on mobilising small savings, wherever possible. This was a relatively less risky venture. The result was the growth in deposits in the rural branches, though not very copious. But then they faced the problem of having very low credit-deposit ratio. Banks came to be criticised for siphoning of rural savings for investment in urban areas. To erase the impression that the banks are in rural areas only to exploit the local economy, the Reserve Bank of India directed them to attain a credit-deposit ratio of 60 per cent in rural and semi-urban branches. This directive induced the bankers to start lending small loans in the rural branches.

Within a short span of time, small loan accounts (amount borrowed being less than Rs.10,000) started growing rapidly in the rural branches. Their number swelled from around 10 lakh on the eve of bank nationalisation to a little more than one crore by 1977. There were very few big borrowing accounts in those days. These small borrowing accounts therefore constituted nearly 90 per cent of the total borrowing accounts handled by the banking sector. In 1983, the definition of small loans was revised, raising the level of credit to Rs.25,000. They continued to grow until the 90s, when the financial sector reforms were introduced. There was a shift in emphasis from social banking to profitable banking. Small accounts and less remunerative transactions almost lost the support of the operational staff. From 1992, there has been a decline both in their number and in their percentage share in the total borrowing accounts. The details are furnished in Table 4.3.

The banking sector at present handles 3.86 crore small borrowing accounts; nearly 47 per cent of them are in the rural areas i.e., 1.72 crore accounts. The amount of credit lent to these accounts is Rs.22,226 crore as on March 2007, the latest available data. With the total number of borrowing accounts rising to 9.44 crore, the number of small borrowers is declining over the years. If in this process, the small borrowers are joining the higher credit brackets, it would be an indication of the growing nexus between the borrowers and the bank. Otherwise, the implications could be ominous from the point of financial inclusion.

Table 4.3

Growth and Decline of Small Loan Accounts

Year	Small* Accounts (No. lakh)	Total Accounts (No. lakh)	Share in Total Accounts (Per cent)
1972	39	43	90.4
1973	42	46	91.8
1974	50	55	90.6
1975	56	62	90.4
1976	77	83	92.5
1977	100	107	93.6
1978	121	130	93.4
1979	143	154	93.1
1980	168	180	93.5
1981	193	207	93.3
1982	219	235	93.1
1983	237	255	92.9
1984	282	295	95.6
1985	321	336	95.7
1986	374	388	96.5
1987	416	434	95.9
1988	459	479	95.8
1989	497	521	95.4
1990	512	538	95.1
1991	588	619	94.9
1992	625	658	95.1
1993	585	621	94.2
1994	558	596	93.6
1995	539	581	92.8
1996	519	566	91.7
1997	501	556	90.1
1998	468	536	87.4
1999	427	523	81.7
2000	393	543	72.3
2001	372	524	71.1
2002	373	564	66.2
2003	369	595	61.9
2004	367	664	55.4
2005	387	771	50.2
2006	384	854	44.9
2007	386	944	40.9
2008	383	10.70	35.8

Note: * Less than Rs.10,000 till 1983; less than Rs.25,000 thereafter.

Source: Basic Statistical Returns of Scheduled Commercial Banks in India, RBI, Mumbai, (various issues).

Differential Rate of Interest Scheme

The Differential Rate of Interest (DRI) Scheme introduced in 1972 was one of the earliest experiments in microcredit. Banks were directed to lend at least 0.5 per cent of their total advances to the poor at an interest rate of 4 per cent. Later in 1978, this limit was raised to one per cent. The interest rate was fixed at two per cent lower than the then prevailing bank rate of 6 per cent. While initially only the public sector banks were directed to implement this scheme, from 1978, private sector banks also agreed to lend under this scheme. The ceiling on advances was fixed at Rs.6500 per borrower. The beneficiaries were the poor from both rural and urban areas. The income criteria adopted for fixing the eligibility was that, in urban areas the family's annual income should be less than Rs.7200 and in rural areas it was to be less than Rs.6400. It was stipulated that 33 per cent (later raised to 40 per cent) of the DRI advances should be made to the borrowers belonging to scheduled classes and scheduled tribes in the villages. To ensure that the benefits of the scheme are made available to the rural borrowers, it was directed that 66 per cent of the advances should be made in rural and semi-urban branches. The progress made was however very poor. In most of the regional consultative committee meetings held periodically in different states under the chairmanship of the Union Finance Minister, banks were cajoled for their failure, if not indifference, to this scheme.

Though this scheme has been in operation for over three decades, the flow of credit under it is unbelievably low. According to the latest data, there are 2.60 lakh borrowing accounts; the amount lent is Rs.634.46 crore accounting for 0.06 per cent of the total credit as on March 2007 (Table 4.4). The number of accounts has been consistently declining from 1991, incidentally after the financial sector reforms were introduced, from 34.49 lakh to less than 3 lakh at present. The amount involved was varying, though the percentage share of the advances under the scheme was consistently moving south.

In the Union Budget of 2007-08, the scope of the scheme was widened raising the ceiling on loan from Rs.6,500 to Rs.15,000 and for housing from Rs.5000 to Rs.20,000. The interest rate, however, remains unchanged at 4 per cent. Some increase in the disbursement is likely to take place as a result. The latest data published in the Statistical Tables Relating to Banks in India 2007 are provisional and there appears to be some discordant movements in the number of accounts and the amount outstanding.

Table 4.4

Advances under Differential Rate of Interest Scheme

Year	Number of Borrowing Accounts (Lakh)	Advances Outstanding (Rs. crore)	Share in Total Advances (Percentage)
1990	37.35	607.24	0.74
1991	34.49	618.82	0.67
1992	31.94	716.25	0.67
1993	29.05	705.33	0.62
1994	24.25	694.18	0.51
1995	19.46	683.03	0.49
1996	15.52	677.66	0.41
1997	14.29	654.76	0.34
1998	9.05	543.65	0.28
1999	7.29	485.00	0.21
2000	5.89	422.00	0.13
2001	5.14	358.00	0.10
2002	n.a.	n.a.	n.a.
2003	3.70	300.00	0.08
2004	3.68	315.00	0.07
2005	3.33	385.27	0.07
2006	3.88	490.22	0.07
2007	2.60	634.46	0.06

Source: Statistical Tables Relating to Banks in India, Reserve Bank of India, Mumbai, (*various issues*).

DRI scheme has been a failure despite the fact that there was neither the funds constraint nor the dearth of the eligible poor. During the last financial year FY2007, the number of DRI borrowing accounts has come down from 3.88 lakh to 2.60 lakh, closing 1.28 lakh accounts, though the amount outstanding has gone up by Rs.144 crore. While the increase may be attributed to the enhancement of housing loan limits, the inference is that the DRI scheme has hardly made any contribution to enhance financial inclusion. Banks could not reach the target of one per cent of the total credit to be lent under this scheme.

5 Recent Initiatives for Financial Inclusion

The broad approach adopted towards financial inclusion in the 1970s and 1980s was more oriented towards expansion of the outreach of banking facilities and meeting the credit requirements of specific sectors and sub-sectors based on the planning priorities. There was hardly any focus on individual or household level inclusion. Though there were programmes to reach the underprivileged segments of population, a sizeable majority of the population particularly vulnerable groups continue to remain excluded from the opportunities and services provided by the financial sector. Under the financial sector reforms during 1990s, the focus of the banking policy was more on creating a strong and globally competitive banking system. In recent years, however, both government and RBI are concerned about the non-availability of banking facilities to the majority of the weaker sections of the society and have undertaken several initiatives towards financial inclusion. In this chapter, an attempt is made briefly to review some of the important initiatives undertaken for financial inclusion in recent years.

NABARD's Initiative in SHG Movement

The SHG-bank linkage programme is a major plank of the strategy for delivering financial services to the poor on a sustainable basis. National Bank for Agriculture and Rural Development (NABARD), as an apex body for agricultural credit, was a pioneer in conceptualising and operationalising SHGs as rural financial intermediaries with the objective of bringing financially excluded people within the fold of the banking sector. It initiated an action research project "Savings and Credit Management of Self-help Groups" in 1987 with the help of an NGO, MYRADA (Mysore Resettlement and Development Agency). Based on the experience gained, the SHG-bank linkage programme was launched by NABARD in 1992 with the policy support of the RBI to provide 'doorstep' banking for the poor. NABARD provides refinance and promotional support to banks for the SHG-Bank linkage programmes. It has developed well-defined guidelines on group formation, size of group, criteria for selection, mode of linkage with banks, linkage models, financial and administrative operations of SHGs and dynamics of group lending (Box 5.1). There is no collateral for bank loan. NABARD provides refinance to the banks to the extent of 100 per cent of the credit provided by them to SHGs.

The SHG-bank linkage programme has made rapid progress since its inception (Table 5.1). As on March 2007, 50 commercial banks, 96 RRBs and 352 cooperative banks were actively participating in the programme. The number of bank branches lending to SHGs was 35294. The SHGs credit linked with banks increased from 4.60 lakh in 2001-02 to 29.30 lakh in 2006-07. The cumulative loan outstanding increased from Rs.1026 crore to Rs.18047 crore during this period. The saving amount outstanding of SHG members with the banks was Rs.2391 crore at the end of March 2007. Assuming that on an average each SHG lends to 14 members, the number of beneficiaries would be about 20 crore and the number of households benefited would be 4.10 crore, assuming average household size of 5 persons. Over 90 per cent of the SHGs linked with banks were found to be exclusive women SHGs; most of them were poor and assetless. Thus, the SHG movement has been instrumental in financial inclusion of women hitherto bypassed by the banking system.

Table 5.1

SHG-Bank Linkage Programme

Year	SHGs Financed during the Year (in Lakh)	Cumulative Number of SHGs Financed (in Lakh)	Bank Loan Outstanding (Rs. Crore)
2001-02	1.98	4.61	1026
2002-03	2.56	7.17	2049
2003-04	3.62	10.79	3904
2004-05	5.39	16.18	6898
2005-06	6.20	22.38	11398
2006-07	6.87	29.25	18047

Source: Progress of SHG-Bank Linkage in India 2006-07, NABARD.

Box 5.1

SHGS-Bank Linkage: Guidelines and Models

Guidelines:

- The membership of the group could vary between 10 and 20.
- The group should be in existence for at least six months with successful savings and credit operations from their own resources.
- The group would be free to decide on selection of borrowers, interest rates and other terms and conditions of loans to members.
- The bank should finance groups as distinct entities, quantum of loan related to savings could be up to 4:1 without any collateral and savings should precede credit in the group.
- Support from voluntary/promotional institutions for group formation, training in group dynamics, accounting, cash management and technical skills should be used.
- The group is expected to meet regularly and all members are expected to participate in decision-making.

Models:

- Model I: SHGs formed and credit linked by banks directly without intervention/facilitation by any NGO. Bank acts as both facilitator and financier.
- Model II: SHGs formed by NGOs and other agencies. After graduation, eligible for bank credit linkage. NGO acts as facilitator and bank as financier.
- Model III: SHGs formed and financed by NGOs directly with finance from banks. NGO acts as facilitator and financial intermediary. Bank lends to NGOs directly.

The region-wise analysis shows that the southern region has achieved remarkable progress in SHG-bank linkage programme from the beginning of the project. Table 5.2 presents region-wise pattern of SHGs linked to banks.

Table 5.2

Regional Distribution of SHGs Linked to Banks

(Percentage)

Region	2001 (End-March)	2006 (End-March)
Northern	3.4	5.9
North-eastern	0.2	2.8
Eastern	8.4	17.6
Central	10.9	12.0
Western	5.9	7.4
Southern	71.1	54.3
All-India	100.0	100.0

Source: Progress of SHG-Bank Linkage in India, NABARD.

The analysis of data in the table reveals that though the geographical disparity has declined over the years, there is still a greater concentration of SHGs linked to banks in southern region. Other two regions, which have significant share in the SHGs linked to banks are eastern and central regions. However, what is noteworthy is that even other regions have made substantial progress and improved their share during this period.

Microfinance and Microfinance Institutions

A new world of microfinance has recently emerged not only as a profitable niche for innovative banking services to the poor but also as a new development initiative for inclusive growth. Microfinance is defined as provision of thrift, credit and other financial services and products of very small amount to the poor in rural, semi-urban or urban areas for enabling them to raise their income levels and improve living standards (NABARD, 1999).[1] Recognising the critical importance of microfinance, a Micro-credit Summit was held in Washington in 1997 attended by the representatives of 137 countries. A campaign was launched as a result for reaching 100 million of the world's poorest families especially women by the year 2005, with microcredit for self-employment and business. In pursuance of this declaration, a number of initiatives have been taken up by the governments, banks and NGOs in the third world countries to enhance the flow of credit and other financial services to the poor.

In India, several NGOs like SEWA, MYRADA, PRADAN, CDF, WWF, Manvodaya, RGVN, DHAN Foundation, Chinmaya Tapovan Trust etc., have initiated programmes for microfinance for the benefit of poor and disadvantaged, particularly women. Though their interventions were successful, the impact remains negligible, considering the magnitude of the problem. Against this background, NABARD has set up a Task Force on microfinance in 1998 to formulate a conceptual and

---

1. Microfinance Regulation Bill defines microfinance services as "providing financial assistance to an individual or an eligible client either directly or through a group mechanism for: (i) an amount not exceeding Rs.50000 in aggregate per individual for small and tiny enterprise, agriculture, allied activities (including for consumption purposes of each individual) or (ii) an amount not exceeding Rs.150000 in aggregate per individual for housing purposes".

policy framework for sustainable growth of microfinance in the country. The Task Force estimated that approximately 7.5 crore of poor households, including 6 crore households in the rural areas, would need microcredit support ranging from Rs.15000 crore to Rs.50000 crore. As against this, the flow of credit from banks and other financial institutions to the weaker sections under various programmes is less than Rs.10000 crore. With such a wide demand and supply gap in micro-credit, innumerable income generating microenterprises remain unexploited in the rural areas.

Based on the recommendations of the Task Force, microfinance has now been recognised as a strategic instrument for poverty alleviation and job creation. SHG-bank linkage is accepted as a core strategy for providing microfinance services to the poor and vulnerable sections of the society. SHG-bank linkage may not have economic impact and cannot be sustainable, unless the programme is linked to microenterprise development for self-employment and increasing the income of the group members.

Microfinance institutions (MFIs), at present, play a significant role in facilitating financial inclusion as they are uniquely positioned in reaching out to the poor and vulnerable section of the society.[2] Since they operate in a limited geographical area, they have a better understanding of the issues specific to the rural poor, enjoy greater acceptability amongst the rural poor and have flexibility in operations providing a level of comfort to their clientele. They are registered as not-for-profit agencies. They depend on borrowed funds from various sources including banks, SIDBI and NABARD. Many banks, particularly private banks, find it easier to lend to MFIs for on-lending to poor. Using MFIs either as a facilitator or as a financial intermediary is definitely an important measure for increasing financial inclusion.

Though there are no reliable data regarding the number of MFIs operating in the country at present, it is roughly estimated that about 1000 NGO-MFIs and more than 20 company MFIs are in the

---

2.   Microfinance Services Regulation Bill defines an MFI as "an organisation or association of individuals established for the purpose of carrying on the business of extending microfinance services. It may include registered society, registered trust and cooperative society."

microfinance field. In Andhra Pradesh, nearly 30000 cooperatives are engaged in microfinance. However, the MFIs are the major players accounting for over 80 per cent of the microfinance portfolio (Government of India, 2008). As on end-March 2006, MFIs disbursed around Rs.3000 crore benefiting more than 83 lakh households.

However, it should be noted that in India, MFIs have not integrated into the mainstream financial market. As a result, most of them have limited resources and lack access to financial resources from the formal financial system. They have also limited opportunities to tap domestic or international funds. Moreover, they suffer from weak management, narrow operational capacity and higher overhead costs. There is also a need for greater legitimacy, accountability and transparency. The proposed Micro Financial Sector (Development and Regulation) Bill when enacted would help in promoting orderly growth of microfinance sector in India.

No-Frills Accounts and Other RBI Initiatives

Although the RBI was concerned about the non-availability of banking facilities to the poor, financial inclusion was explicitly used as a policy objective and thrust of banking policy only in the beginning of April 2005. Several policy initiatives were recently introduced aiming at promoting financial inclusion of underprivileged and vulnerable section of the society. The RBI Annual Policy Statement for 2005-06 announced that:

- RBI will implement policies to encourage banks which provide extensive services, while disincentivising those which are not responsive to the banking needs of the community, including the underprivileged.

- The nature, scope and cost of services will be monitored to assess whether there is any denial, implicit or explicit, of basic banking services to the common person.

- Banks are urged to review their existing practices to align them with the objective of financial inclusion.

Some of the major initiatives implemented are the following:

No-frills Accounts: The banks were advised in November 2005 to offer basic banking no-frills accounts, either with nil or very low minimum balances as well as charges, which would enable hitherto, excluded people to access easily bank services. The low cost or free of cost account is intentionally introduced to expand the outreach of such accounts to vast section of the population having low income. Most of the banks have already introduced the scheme of no-frills accounts and there has been a significant progress in the number of accounts opened by them. As on December 2008, the number of no-frills accounts opened were 2.82 crore.

Simple KYC Norms: In order to ensure that persons belonging to low-income groups, both in urban and rural areas do not encounter difficulties in opening bank accounts, the Know Your Customer (KYC) procedure for opening new accounts was simplified for those accounts with balances not exceeding Rs.50000 and credit limits not exceeding Rs.100000 in a year. The simplified procedure allowed introduction by a customer on whom the full KYC drill had already been done.

General Credit Card (GCC): Banks have been asked to consider general purpose credit card facility up to Rs.25000 at their rural and semi-urban branches for rural people, particularly the landless class. The GCC is in the nature of revolving credit, entitling the holder to withdraw up to the limit sanctioned. The limits are based on an assessment of household cash flows without insistence on security or purpose of credit. The interest rate on the facility is completely deregulated and 50 per cent of the GCC loans are treated as priority sector lending.

Adoption of Districts for 100 Per cent Financial Inclusion: In order to ensure 100 per cent financial inclusion, the state level bankers' committees (SLBC) were advised to identify one or more districts for adoption by banks for financial inclusion. In the identified districts, surveys were conducted to identify households without bank accounts. Responsibility was given to banks in the area for ensuring that all those who wanted to have a bank account to be provided with one by allocating the villages among the different banks. The bank staff or their agents, who are usually local NGOs or village volunteers, contact the households at their doorstep. The banks in association with insurance companies also provide innovative insurance policies at affordable cost, covering life disability and health cover. SHGs and MFIs are also used extensively for financial inclusion on the credit side.

Many of the SLBCs have reported having achieved 100 per cent financial inclusion in 134 districts, as on 2008. The RBI is undertaking an evaluation of the progress made in these districts by an independent external agency to draw lessons for further action in this regard. In order to improve financial inclusion in eastern and north-eastern regions, the RBI has set up a Committee on Financial Sector Plan headed by the Deputy Governor with members from banks and other financial institutions and state governments for expanding banking facilities and formulating area-specific action plans for accelerating financial inclusion.

Business Facilitator and Business Correspondence Models: In January 2006, the RBI permitted banks to utilise the services of NGOs/ SHGs, MFIs and other civil society organisations as intermediaries for providing financial and banking services through the use of business facilitator (BF) and business correspondent (BC) models. The BC models allow banks to undertake doorstep banking in rural areas. In April 2008, banks were permitted to engage retired bank employees, ex-servicemen and government employees as BCs subject to appropriate due diligence. Banks were also allowed to use post office network as BCs to increase their outreach.

Use of ICT Solutions: Technology can play an important role in reducing transaction cost of providing banking services particularly in rural areas and for low-income group segments. The RBI has encouraged banks to use ICT solutions for enhancing their outreach with the help of their BCs. Three types of technologies have been identified: (i) pro-poor new information and communication technology, primarily low-cost cell phones; (ii) ATMs and other point of sales devices; and (iii) smart plastic cards. Mobile phone-based services are revolutionising microfinance services in a number of countries. Banks in India have initiated pilot projects using smart cards and mobile technology to increase outreach. Biometric-enabled devices for uniquely identifying customers are also being increasingly adopted. Use of ICT solutions also led some banks to adopt branchless banking for delivery of banking services at affordable price and to a wider section of the population.

Financial Literacy and Credit Counseling: Recognising that the lack of awareness is a major factor for financial exclusion, RBI has initiated a number of measures for increasing financial literacy and credit counseling. It has set up a multilingual website in 13 languages on all matters concerning banking. Financial literacy programmes are being launched in each state with the active involvement of state governments. SLBCs were asked to set up a credit counseling centre in one district as pilot and extend it to all other districts in due course. There is also plan to set up a centre for financial education & excellence in RBI's College of Agricultural Banking at Pune.

National Rural Financial Inclusion Plan

Notwithstanding all the initiatives taken so far, a sizeable majority of the population at the bottom of the pyramid continues to remain excluded from the opportunities and services provided by the financial sector. With a view to correct this situation and extend the reach of the financial sector to such groups by minimising the barriers to access, the Government of India constituted a "Committee on Financial Inclusion" on 22 June 2006. The Committee reviewed the various dimensions of financial inclusion in depth and viewed it as a comprehensive and holistic process of ensuring access to financial services and timely and adequate credit, particularly for the vulnerable groups such as weaker sections and low-income groups at affordable costs. In order to widen the outreach of financial services and build an inclusive financial sector, the Committee has suggested an overall strategy based on:

- Effecting improvements within the existing formal credit delivery mechanism;

- Undertaking measures to improve credit absorption capacity especially amongst marginal and sub-marginal farmers and poor non-cultivator households;

- Evolving innovative new models for effective outreach;

- Leveraging on technology based-solutions.

Following this strategy and keeping in view the enormity of the task involved, the Committee recommended taking up on a mission mode, a National Rural Financial Inclusion Plan (NRFIP). The plan has set targets to increase financial inclusion in the country across regions and across institutions. The following are the targets and recommendations to achieve the same:

- A target of providing access to comprehensive financial services to at least 50 per cent (55.77 million) of the financially excluded rural households by 2012 and the remaining by 2015.

- Rural and semi-urban commercial bank branches and RRBs should cover a minimum of 250 new cultivator and non-cultivator households per branch per annum, with emphasis on financing marginal farmers and poor non-cultivator households.

- The government should constitute a national mission on financial inclusion comprising representatives of all stakeholders for suggesting overall policy changes required and ensuring achievement of universal financial inclusion within a specific timeframe.

- RRBs should be made vehicles to widen and deepen the process of financial inclusion. This require recapitalisation of RRBs with negative net worth, widening of their network to cover all unbanked villages in the district where they are operating, either by opening a branch or through BF/BC model in a time-bound manner, separate credit plans for excluded regions and strengthening governance with strong rural orientation. Ultimately the banks should endeavour to have a BC touch point riding on appropriate technology in each of the six lakh villages.

- The government should constitute two funds with NABARD: financial inclusion & development fund for promotional and development initiatives and financial inclusion technology fund for application of ICT, with an initial corpus of Rs.500 crore each to be contributed by Government of India, RBI and NABARD.

- Microcredit should be linked with micro-insurance and hence micro-insurance needs further push and guidance from both government and regulator.

The Committee has also made specific recommendations to encourage SHGs in excluded regions, legal status for SHGs and strengthening primary cooperatives for financial inclusion given their extensive outreach. The Government of India in the Union Budget 2005-06 has accepted the recommendations of the Committee to create two funds—financial inclusion fund and financial inclusion technology fund.

Status Report on Banking in the Southern States

As adumbrated in the previous chapters, at present, secondary macro data available are only on indicators of depth and efficiency of the financial system, working of financial market, sectoral allocation of resources etc. Detailed empirical data are not available on access to finance, available range of financial services, how inclusive financial system are and who has access to which financial services. Until recently, there has been little systematic information on who is served by the financial sector, which financial institutions or services are the most effective at supporting access to poor households, and what are the barriers to the expansion of financial outreach. Whatever limited data available, the focus was more on firm and sectoral level access rather than household level. Household surveys are required to compile detailed information on who use which financial services from which type of institutions and socioeconomic profile of households, that are financially included or excluded.

After analysing the macro level data on financial inclusion/ exclusion, this study has made an attempt to carry out a comprehensive household survey in different states in the southern region to assess the various dimensions of financial inclusion/exclusion. The salient features of the states, districts and villages selected for the field study are highlighted in this chapter as a backdrop for the field level findings.

Banking Development in Selected States

The four southern states—Andhra Pradesh, Karnataka, Kerala and Tamil Nadu—have a fairly well-developed banking sector, having a long history of over a century. Banks' penetration into the rural areas is more pronounced in all these states compared to the rest of India. Small private sector banks were in existence in a large number of villages in these states, more particularly, in Karnataka and Kerala, for fairly long periods (Thingalaya, 2009b). In their own way, they have served generations of customers within their own areas of operation. Karnataka has two banks, which have completed centuries. Tamil Nadu also has two century-old banks, one in the public sector and another in the private sector. State Bank of India, in its previous incarnation as Bank of Madras (besides Bank of Bengal and Bank of Bombay) was operating since 1843. Kerala also had a hundred year old local bank till recently.

Gramin banks are omnipresent in these states, with Karnataka and Andhra Pradesh in the lead. These are the two states, which have taken the initiative to promote *gramin* banks to cover the entire states, unlike many other states. After the recent merger of *gramin* banks, their number has come down to 5 and 6 respectively in these two states. In Kerala, the number has remained unchanged at 2, while in Tamil Nadu it has reduced from 3 to 2. The details of the amalgamated *gramin* banks in the four states are given in Annexure A-3.

Among the four states, Andhra Pradesh was not very active in promoting banking companies. Only 20 banks could originate from this state and only two among them have survived. Andhra Bank is the oldest bank followed by State Bank of Hyderabad. In the 70s, when the invention of *gramin* banks was made, 16 of them appeared in different districts of the state, thanks to the proactive role played by the Government of India, the state government and 5 public sector banks. In Karnataka, 13 *gramin* banks were established by 6 public sector banks. Another species of banks, which came up in the late 90s is the local area bank. Two banks of this type have found shelter in the state, supported by local initiative. They are: Coastal Local Area Bank Ltd. and Krishna Bhima Samruddhi Local Area Bank Ltd. The former is located in Vijayawada and has branches in Krishna, Guntur and West Godavari districts. Krishna Bhima Samruddhi Local Area Bank Ltd., though located in Mahbubnagar in Andhra Pradesh, has branches in Gulbarga and Raichur districts of Karnataka also. Both the banks have very small volumes of business.

Karnataka has produced 78 banks, beginning with Chitradurga Bank Ltd. established in 1870 in a small town, Chitradurga, not far from

Bangalore. The next bank came up in a much smaller temple town near Mysore, Nanjangud in 1885—Nanjangud Srikanteshvara Bank Ltd., Bangalore had to wait till 1890 to get its own bank, Bangalore Union Bank Ltd., which remained in business for half a century. The more durable banks like Canara Bank and Corporation Bank came up in 1906 in South Kanara district, the nursery of banking. Syndicate Bank joined them later in 1925. Mangalore, a coastal town gained prominence with banks like Vijaya Bank Ltd. and Karnataka Bank Ltd. which started growing here. Syndicate Bank was a pioneer in rural banking. It had opened 25 rural branches in South Kanara district as early as in 1946. Though a few of them were closed later for some years, the awareness about banking facilities were created by them nearly half a century ago in the villages. Five public sector banks—Canara Bank, Syndicate Bank, Corporation Bank, Vijaya Bank and State Bank of Mysore as well as two private sector banks—Karnataka Bank Ltd. and ING Vysya Bank Ltd. originating from the state have developed a strong banking base in the state.

Kerala has the second largest number of banks, beginning with Trivandrum Permanent Bank Ltd. established in 1899. As many as 118 banks were born in the state since then. Besides them, two regional rural banks have appeared on the scene in 1976. The oldest bank did not live beyond six decades as it was merged with Canara Bank in 1961. The other century-old bank, Nedungadi Bank Ltd., born in Calicut in 1899 was merged with Punjab National Bank in 2003. Four banks in the private sector—Federal Bank Ltd., Catholic Syrian Bank Ltd., South Indian Bank Ltd., and Dhanalakshmi Bank Ltd., have been operating in smaller towns for over five decades besides the State Bank of Travancore, which was established in 1946.

Tamil Nadu has produced the largest number of banks 149, though only six of them could retain their individual identity over the years. The oldest bank born in the state was the Bank of Madras, established in 1843. It was patterned after the other two Presidency banks, Bank of Calcutta and Bank of Bombay already existing then. In the case of Bank of Madras, out of the capital of Rs.30 lakh, the share of the Government was Rs.3 lakh—"the Governor in Council of Fort St. George for the time being on behalf of the East India Company holding 300 shares of

Rs.1000 each". Merging the three Presidency banks in 1921, Imperial Bank of India was formed. After Independence, its reincarnation was as State Bank of India, owned by the Reserve Bank of India. During 2007, the Government of India has taken over its ownership from the Reserve Bank of India. Two nationalised banks having wide presence in the state are Indian Bank and Indian Overseas Bank. There are four other home-grown private sector banks having large branch network. They are the century-old City Union Bank Ltd., Karur Vysya Bank Ltd., Lakshmi Vilas Bank Ltd., and Tamilnad Mercantile Bank Ltd.

The details of the volume of business handled by banks in the four states are furnished in Table 6.1.

Andhra Pradesh has the largest branch network and Kerala has the smallest among the four states. In rural banking also Andhra Pradesh has a better record of performance. It has not only a larger network of rural branches, but also a wider customer base in the rural areas. It has 1.38 crore rural deposit accounts and the share of rural deposits is more than 11 per cent of the state's total bank deposits.

Karnataka has the second largest number of rural branches and has nearly one crore of rural deposit accounts. It has larger volume of rural deposits than the other three states. Banks in Tamil Nadu handle the largest volume of advances and they also have a bigger base of borrowing customers.

Banking Profiles of the Selected Districts

The banking profiles of the four selected districts are presented with special reference to the pattern of banking development prevailing in them. It is more of a quantitative assessment, providing a comparative picture of the four districts. The pattern of development varies widely among them, with Udupi district on the one extreme and Madurai district on the other end. The former has made excellent progress in rural banking while the more prosperous district in Tamil Nadu lags behind visibly. Some of the relevant banking data are furnished in Table 6.2.

Table 6.1

Banking Profiles of the Southern States

States	Rural Branches (number)	Total Branches (number)	Rural Deposit Accounts (No.lakh)	Rural Deposit Amount (Rs.crore)	Total Deposit Accounts (No.lakh)	Total Deposit Amount (Rs. crore)	Total Borrowing Accounts (No.lakh)	Total Credit (Rs. crore)
Andhra Pradesh	2289	6240	138.16	18,342	501.94	1,78,647	118.30	1,61,552
Karnataka	2122	5666	110.94	18,200	390.80	2,00,609	78.68	1,63,788
Kerala	327	4007	19.71	4,588	274.49	1,09,919	56.79	69,689
Tamil Nadu	1650	5716	92.18	18,975	452.57	1,98,554	142.84	2,27,686

Source: Basic Statistical Returns of Scheduled Commercial Banks in India, 2008, Reserve Bank of India, Mumbai.

Table 6.2

Banking Profiles of the Selected Districts

District	Rural Branches (number)	Total Branches (number)	Rural Deposit Accounts (No.lakh)	Rural Deposit Amount (Rs.crore)	Total Deposit Accounts (No.lakh)	Total Deposit Amount (Rs.crore)	Total Borrowing Accounts (No.lakh)	Total Credit (Rs.crore)
Anantapur	104	250	8.99	770.31	26.31	4696.27	7.52	3196.47
Udupi	130	238	9.30	2068.46	17.76	5660.54	1.80	2548.76
Kasaragod	26	137	1.83	195.11	10.02	1789.17	2.45	1477.79
Madurai	54	255	3.35	521.10	20.87	6788.58	6.23	6972.25

Source: Basic Statistical Returns of Scheduled Commercial Banks in India, 2008, Reserve Bank of India, Mumbai.

Anantapur District in Andhra Pradesh

Anantapur district has 250 branches of commercial banks, of which 104 are located in rural areas. Syndicate Bank is the lead bank of the district, having 33 branches. Andhra Pragathi Grameena Bank is the regional rural bank operating in the district. It has the largest network of branches 85 in the district. Two other banks having major presence in the district are State Bank of India (34 branches) and Andhra Bank (25 branches). Smaller banks of the private sector like Karur Vysya Bank Ltd., ING Vysya Bank Ltd., City Union Bank Ltd., and Karnataka Bank Ltd. also operate here. In the district headquarter there are the branches of ICICI Bank Ltd., HDFC Bank Ltd., and IndusInd Bank Ltd.

The earliest bank to open a branch in the district is Syndicate Bank, which opened its branch in Hindupur in 1937 and in Anantapur town in 1941. After the bank was designated as the lead bank in 1969, it conducted the survey of unbanked centres in the district and paved the way for many banks to open their branches in the identified unbanked villages.

Anantapur District Central Cooperative Bank Ltd., one of the oldest cooperative institutions in the district has 19 branches. Its market share in total deposits mobilised in the district, however, is negligible (2 per cent). Its share in total credit is 15 per cent according to the Annual Credit Plan 2008-09.

Rural branches of all banks have 8.99 lakh deposit accounts, having mobilised Rs.770.31 crore of rural savings. The total number of deposit accounts handled by all the banks in the district is 26.31 lakh, the highest among the selected districts.

Udupi District in Karnataka

Udupi district is one of the highly banked districts in the country. It was a part of the South Kanara district, which is considered as the cradle of banking. The new district came into being in 1997. Syndicate Bank was designated as the lead bank for the undivided district in 1969. After the formation of the new district, Syndicate Bank was designated as the lead bank for the new district also. It has 69 branches in the district.

Of the total number of 238 branches in the new district, 130 are operating in rural areas. They have canvassed 9.30 lakh deposit accounts in these branches. The amount of rural deposits mobilised is the highest among all the four districts selected—Rs.2068.46 crore. Nearly 28 per cent of the total deposit of the district is mobilised from the rural areas. Karnataka Vikas Grameena Bank is the regional rural bank operating in the district with 11 branches, accounting for a major share of the district's banking business.

It may be worth mentioning here that Udupi district has the advantage of having banking facilities for more than a century. Corporation Bank was born in 1906 in Udupi, then a small temple town; Canara Bank has a branch in Karkala, a *taluk* headquarter, since 1926. Many other villages, like Bailur, Barkur, Basrur, Byndoor, Gangulli, Hebri, Nitte, Palimar, Perdoor and Saligrama are having the branches of Syndicate Bank since 1946. These villages are having banking facilities for more than half a century. Along with 14 public sector banks, there are the branches of ICICI Bank Ltd., Axis Bank Ltd., HDFC Bank Ltd., and ING Vysya Bank Ltd. operating in Udupi. The latest additions are the branches of United Bank of India and Oriental Bank of Commerce.

In the cooperative sector, the South Canara District Central Cooperative Bank Ltd. has 20 branches in the district and its share in the total district credit plan is 11 per cent. According to the 2001 Census data, Udupi district has one of the highest banking penetration ratios in India, 78 per cent. The national average ratio is 35 per cent.

Kasaragod District in Kerala

This small district in north Kerala has the smallest number of bank branches: 137. As most of the villages in the state are very large, they qualify to be classified as semi-urban areas. Hence, the number of rural branches is very small. They are only 26. The number of deposit accounts serviced by them is also one of the smallest: 1.83 lakh and the amount of deposits mobilised is not more than Rs.195.11 crore.

Prior to 1956, when the states were reorganised on a linguistic basis, Kasaragod district was a part of the undivided South Kanara district. The first bank to open a branch in the present boundaries of the new district was Syndicate Bank. It opened a branch in Kasaragod town in 1936. Jaya Laxmi Bank Ltd., a Mangalore-based bank, which later merged with Vijaya Bank in 1967, opened a branch here in 1939.

Syndicate Bank, the lead bank of the district has 17 branches. The regional rural bank sponsored by it, North Malabar Gramin Bank is operating in the district since 1976. It has 48 branches, spread throughout the district. It is the major provider of credit, having an outstanding level of credit of Rs.401.97 crore. Incidentally, it operates with a credit-deposit ratio of 153 per cent as on March 2007. Vijaya Bank is the other public sector bank having the third largest number of branches, 13. Besides 16 public sector banks having their branches in the district, three of the new generation banks and three of the Kerala-based private sector banks have their presence in the district.

Kasaragod District Cooperative Central Bank Ltd. has a significant presence in the district with 88 branches.

Madurai District in Tamil Nadu

Madurai is one of the more prosperous districts in Tamil Nadu. In terms of the volume of banking business, it stands first among the four selected districts. In rural banking, however, the district is not in the forefront. Out of 255 branches only 54 are operating in the rural areas. They could reach out to only 3.35 lakh deposit-account holders. Hardly 7 per cent of the total bank deposit originates from the rural branches.

Madurai district has seen the birth of two local banks established in the forties. Bank of Madurai Ltd. was born in 1943. It was in existence till 2001, when it was taken over by ICICI Bank Ltd. Through this process, some of the branches of Bank of Madurai Ltd. became the branches of the aggressive private sector bank. Pandyan Grama Bank Ltd. was the other bank born in Madurai in 1946. It was merged with Canara Bank in 1963, when merger of weaker banks with bigger banks was encouraged by the Reserve Bank of India. As a result of this merger, Canara Bank has acquired a wider base in the district. Syndicate Bank entered the district in 1966.

The banking sector in the district has mobilised an amount of Rs.6788 crore as deposits. Its advances are more than the deposits; Rs.6972 crore as is the case with the banking sector in Tamil Nadu, where traditionally the credit-deposit ratio remains above 100 per cent. Madurai city is ranked 28th among the top 100 banking centres in India, in terms of the total amount of credit deployed.

Canara Bank is the lead bank of the district and has 29 branches in different parts of the district. State Bank of India has a network of 31 branches. Pandyan Grama Bank, sponsored by Indian Overseas Bank operates in the district, having 5 branches.

Salient Features of the Selected Villages

Some of the important features of the four selected villages from the four southern states are provided below. These selected villages are different from each other in many aspects. Two of them are banked villages: Kedinje village in Karnataka and Kayyar in Kerala. The other two villages, Nadimipalli village in Andhra Pradesh and Kundukulam village in Tamil Nadu do not have any bank branch in the vicinity. Kedinje is having a branch of a nationalised bank, Canara Bank and this village is located on the main road. The village from Kerala, located in the interior, has the branch of a *gramin* bank, North Malabar Gramin Bank. The other two villages from Andhra Pradesh and Tamil Nadu are unbanked villages.

Nadimipalli

This is a small village in the interior located in Narpala *mandal*. With only 131 households, it has a fairly prosperous agricultural sector, growing cash crop like banana. Tempos and trucks carry the banana crop to Anantapur and even to Bangalore, where there is a good market. The village is electrified and has a primary school and drinking water facility is also available.

Banking facilities are available in Narpala town, where State Bank of India has a branch besides the branch of Andhra Pragathi Grameena Bank, the latter is operating here since 1998. The service area of the *gramin* bank includes two villages: H. Sadhana Palli and Mangapatnam hamlet. Nadimipalli branch does not come under its command area.

Kedinje

Kedinje village is located in Karkala *taluk*, one of the highly banked *taluks* in Karnataka. This small *taluk* is far ahead of many bigger towns in India in terms of financial inclusion. Banking services have reached 80 per cent of the households in Karkala *taluk* according to Census of India 2001, *Karnataka: Tables on Houses, Household Amenities and Assets*. There 43 branches of different banks in the *taluk*. Karkala *taluk* has attained such a high level of financial inclusion much before the need for financial inclusion was recognised and emphasised by the Reserve Bank of India. Banks here have developed a highway for rural banking on their own, not directed by the regulator or the owners. And this is a unique achievement of banks, which has perhaps no parallel elsewhere.

Kedinje is located on the state highway called Kudremukh road, linking NH17 and NH13. On this road of 27 kms, there are nine rural branches—one rural branch at every three kms, one of the rarest instances of banking concentration. Kedinje village is having Canara Bank's branch since 1974. South Canara District Central Cooperative Bank Ltd. came here in 2006. This village has been designated as the *Bima Grama* by Life Insurance Corporation of India along with other adjoining villages Kalya in December 2003. Besides banking, insurance also has made good progress in this village. A good number of auto-*rickshaws*, many small tempos are always found on the main road. There is a rice mill here and in another three kms, there is a cashew-nut processing unit. The village is electrified and has a high school, which is more than 50 years old.

Kayyar

Kayyar village in Kasaragod *taluk* is situated off the National Highway 17 on the road linking Uppala to Puttur in the east. Having a population of 1255 persons, it is fairly prosperous with some families having one or other member working in the Gulf. Prosperity of the village is reflected in the good number of independent bungalows with big gates abutting the road. It has drinking water facility, has a post office and a primary school as well.

A branch of North Malabar Gramin Bank is operating in Jodukallu, which comes under Paivalike *panchayat*. This branch has been functioning here since 1978. Syndicate Bank, the lead bank of the district, has a branch at Paivalike. South Indian Bank Ltd., a Kerala based private sector bank has a branch at Pachambala.

Kundukulam

This is a relatively less developed village from Thirumangala block. The total population is 1038, where males outnumber females, unlike in the other three villages. Literacy ratio is one of the lowest. The block has one of the highest number of marginal farmers, cultivating farm holdings of less than one hectare. There are 27,531 such holdings in the block.

This block has the lowest number of bank branches among the 13 blocks in the district. There are only five branches of commercial banks and only two branches of cooperative banks for a population of 1,82,472. Population per branch works out to be 36,494 as against the national average of 16,000 persons per branch.

Field Study Design and Methodology

The process of financial inclusion at household level takes place in a given contiguous geographical area or a command area of a bank branch or any financial institution network. The dynamics of the process of financial inclusion and factors affecting the same can be meaningfully looked into only if all the households in a given village are included in the field study. Hence, instead of sampling technique, an empirical study of all households in a given village in the command area of a bank branch is ideally more revealing and appropriate for this type of study. Accordingly, the study has adopted census of all households of selected villages instead of random sample study of households. It should, however, be noted that though the findings of the field study are quite revealing and provide useful policy implications, they should not be construed to represent for the states, where the villages studied are located.

As already discussed, four villages were selected on random basis in four districts in consultation with the concerned lead banks. The salient features of the districts and villages selected are already explained above. Field survey was carried out on a rapid appraisal basis during 2008-09 by a team comprising the faculty of the institute and NGOs in the area selected for the purpose. The data were collected through structured schedule, which is tested on pilot basis. The number of households of villages selected from the four districts and states is given in Table 6.3.

Table 6.3

The Villages Selected in Four States

States	Districts Selected	Census Villages	Number of Households
Andhra Pradesh	Anantapur	Nadimipalli	131
Karnataka	Udupi	Kedinje	162
Kerala	Kasaragod	Kayyar	250
Tamil Nadu	Madurai	Kundukulam	187
Total			730

Source: Field survey data.

In all, 730 households were studied. It may be noted that access to financial services is required not only by the households but also by eligible members of the households. The total number of members of the households in the selected villages is 2600. The number of households studied varies widely as it depends on the total number of households in the villages selected. To supplement the survey data, the study has also adopted consultation and participatory approach to gather information on financial inclusion from the financial institutions concerned. The study team also held detailed discussion with the officials of lead bank and bank branches in the area.

The analytical framework adopted is mainly governed by the primary objective of the study, which is to assess the financial inclusion/exclusion in all aspects. No sophisticated statistical analysis has been carried out; instead only cross section and disaggregated analysis of data of financially included and financially excluded households has been made to bring out the implications.

7 | Financial Inclusion

Field Data Analysis

In the ultimate analysis, while studying financial inclusion, it is important to know empirically who have access to which finance services and who are excluded from these, what is their socioeconomic status and what barriers they confront in accessing finance from the financial institutions. The field data analysis in this chapter, therefore, mainly focuses on the:

1. Study of the pattern of inclusion/exclusion of households from access to financial services in different regional background.

2. Disaggregation of financially included/excluded by gender, occupational structure, education, income groups and other socioeconomic characteristics.

3. An analysis of the pattern of utilisation of financial services from different type of institutions.

4. Identification of the barriers confronted by the households in accessing financial services, and

5. An appraisal of the perception of households on the support needed to improve access to financial services.

Extent of Financial Inclusion/Exclusion

At the outset, it is important to know the extent of financial inclusion/ exclusion among the total households studied in the villages selected in different states. Financial inclusion is defined, for the purpose of survey, any household members having bank account, either savings or loan, with any formal financial institution. Financially excluded are those who do not have any accounts with the formal financial institutions. Table 7.1 sets out the extent of financial inclusion and exclusion in the selected villages in different states.

Table 7.1

Financially Included and Financially Excluded Households

State	Total Respondents (Number)	Financially Included		Financially Excluded	
		Number	*Per cent*	*Number*	*Per cent*
Andhra Pradesh	131	113	86.26	18	13.74
Karnataka	162	139	85.80	23	14.20
Kerala	250	223	89.20	27	10.80
Tamil Nadu	187	86	45.99	101	54.01
Total	730	561	76.85	169	23.15

Source: Field survey data.

It is evident from the data in the table that there is a wide variation in the pattern of financial inclusion and exclusion in different villages in different states. Financial inclusion varies from 86 per cent in Andhra Pradesh village to 46 per cent in Tamil Nadu village. The extent of financial exclusion is the highest in Tamil Nadu (54 per cent) and the lowest in Kerala (11 per cent). In Andhra Pradesh, out of 131 households in the village studied, 113 have reported availing banking facilities, which works out to 86 per cent financially included. Financially excluded are only 18 households (14 per cent). In Kerala, out of 250 households studied, 223 or 89 per cent have banking account and 27 or 11 per cent have no banking account. Similarly, in the Karnataka village, out of 162 households, 139 (86 per cent) have reported banking accounts and the balance 23 households (14 per cent) were found in the financial exclusion group. Tamil Nadu village has the lowest financial inclusion (46 per cent). Out of 187 households, 101 households (54 per cent) are found financially excluded.

Awareness of Availability of Financial Services

It is important to know whether the households studied are aware of the availability of various financial products and services. Awareness is an important element of financial literacy. The lack of awareness or knowing the availability of financial services in terms of location and type of services is considered as one of the main barriers on the demand-side for expanding financial inclusion particularly among the illiterate, poor and vulnerable segments of the society in rural areas. Unless the households are made aware of the availability of various financial products and services, they would not be motivated to come forward to avail them from the financial institutions. The process of financial inclusion, in fact, begins with creating awareness of the existence of financial institution, availability of various financial products and services, terms and conditions in which they are available and the benefits that can be derived from their use. In the Indian rural setting, all these constitute integral part of financial literacy.

Recognising the critical importance of awareness in the promotion of financial inclusion, field data were collected and compiled on awareness of various financial products and services, which are presented in Table 7.2.

It is interesting to note that in the selected villages in Andhra Pradesh, Karnataka and Kerala, almost all households studied have reported their awareness of the existence of bank branch in their village or in the proximity to their village. However, in Tamil Nadu village, nearly half of the households interviewed have reported their ignorance about the existence of a bank branch in the nearby areas. A similar pattern of response is also observed in the case of awareness of saving facility and awareness of loan facility. More than 80 per cent of the respondents from the three villages in Andhra Pradesh, Karnataka and Kerala have reported awareness of the availability of saving and loan facilities with the bank branch in their neighbourhood. Contrary to this, about 52 per cent of the households in the village selected from Tamil Nadu are not aware of the availability of saving facilities with the bank, while in the case of the availability of loan facility, nearly three-fourths of the households have responded positively.

As regards awareness of money transfer facility, except Karnataka village, in all other three villages, the response pattern is more or less the same. While in Karnataka village, 47 per cent of the households studied are aware of the money transfer facility with the bank, in the other three villages, less than one-fourth of the households reported its awareness. In the case of insurance, only in Andhra village, 62 per cent of the households studied have reported their awareness. In the case of Karnataka and Kerala villages, the percentages of households reporting

Table 7.2

Awareness of Availability of Financial Services

Financial Products/Services	Nadimipalli (AP)		Kedinje (Karnataka)		Kayyar (Kerala)		Kundukulam (Tamil Nadu)		Total	
	No.	%	No.	%	No.	%	No.	%	No.	%
Existence of bank branch	121	92.36	159	98.15	243	97.20	94	50.27	617	84.52
Awareness of saving facility	110	83.97	148	91.36	204	81.60	89	47.59	551	75.48
Awareness of loan facility	119	90.84	152	93.83	238	95.20	142	75.94	651	89.18
Awareness of money transfer	33	25.19	76	46.91	52	20.80	36	19.25	197	26.98
Awareness of insurance	81	61.83	69	42.59	118	47.20	66	35.29	334	45.75
Awareness of mutual funds	2	1.52	19	11.73	32	12.80	8	4.28	61	8.36
Awareness of collection of cheques/bills	33	25.19	81	50.00	160	64.00	62	33.16	336	46.03
Awareness of other banking facilities	0	0	36	22.22	0	0	1	0.53	37	5.07
Not aware (any one)	10	7.63	3	1.85	7	2.80	45	24.06	65	8.90

Source: Field survey data.

awareness works out to 43 and 47 respectively. Tamil Nadu village has the lowest percentage of insurance awareness among the households (35). The majority of the households studied in all the four villages are not aware of the mutual fund facility. In Andhra village, only 2 out of 131 households have reported to be aware of it. In Tamil Nadu village, only 8 out of 187 households are aware of the mutual fund facility. In Karnataka and Kerala villages, the position is slightly better; nearly 12 per cent of households are aware of this financial product.

Regarding the facility of collection of cheques and bills, whereas in Karnataka and Kerala villages, slightly more than 50 per cent of the households are aware of the availability of these facilities, in Andhra village, the percentage of households reported awareness of these facilities are only 25 per cent and in Tamil Nadu, only 33 per cent. The households, who are ignorant of the availability of any banking facility are only few except in Tamil Nadu village, where 24 per cent of the households belonged to this category. Thus, the analysis of data in Table 7.2 shows that financial literacy status at household level in rural areas in Karnataka, Kerala and Andhra Pradesh is relatively better in all aspects than in Tamil Nadu.

Access to Financial Services

Access to finance contributes to household entry, empowerment and consequently to improvement in income. Conceptually, access has many dimensions on demand-side including awareness, acquaintance or understanding the usage of various financial products and services. Access is also governed by supply-side factors such as price and non-price barriers. Services need to be available when and where demanded, and products need to be tailored to specific requirements. There are also differences between access and usage of products and services. Even if the customers have complete knowledge of all financial products and services and capability to avail them, some of them may not be inclined to use the same. In other words, they have access, but they are non-users. They are voluntarily excluded. From the policy point of view, they are not a problem. The aim of financial inclusion is more concerned with those, who are willing to use and badly needed financial services but have access problem.

The field study is mainly centred around on demand-side dimension of access and respondents are asked to ascertain whether they have access and can avail different financial products and services. In Table 7.3, responses received are analysed for different products and services. The analysis of the data discloses wide differences in access problems in different villages and for different products. As regards savings and loan products, majority of the respondents have no access problems in Andhra Pradesh, Karnataka and Kerala villages, while in the Tamil Nadu case, more than half of the respondents have access problems for these products; out of 187 respondents only 48 per cent have access to saving facility and 30 per cent to loan facility. In the Andhra village, the percentage of households having access to saving facilities is less than the percentage of households having access to loan facilities. In other villages also, the percentage of households having access to saving facilities are more than the percentage of households having access to loan facilities.

As regards access to other financial products/services, while in Andhra village, 62 per cent of the households studied have indicated access to Kisan Credit Cards, in other villages, only few households have reported access to these cards. In the case of all other financial products and services except for insurance, the majority of the households have indicated access problems. In the case of insurance, nearly one-third of the households have reported access and two-thirds have access problems.

While the number of households who have reported that they do not have access to any one of financial products/services are very few in Andhra village (8), Karnataka (18), and Kerala (7), in Tamil Nadu village their number is 63; nearly one-third of the households studied. This has serious implications as regards financial inclusion is concerned.

Table 7.4 provides the details of the sources of information, which led the households to the entry into the financial sector.

It is important to note that financial institutions like banks and insurance companies do not seem to have played any role in improving access and thereby promoting financial inclusion. Only in Andhra Pradesh and Karnataka villages, about 36 per cent of the households have reported bank employee/insurance agent as their source of

Table 7.3

Access to and Availability of Financial Services

Financial Products/Services	Nadimipalli (AP)		Kedinje (Karnataka)		Kayyar (Kerala)		Kundukulam (Tamil Nadu)		Total	
	No.	%	No.	%	No.	%	No.	%	No.	%
Savings accounts	102	77.9	131	80.9	183	73.2	89	47.6	505	69.2
Loans	111	84.7	95	58.6	126	50.4	56	29.9	388	53.2
Kisan credit card	81	61.8	3	1.9	19	7.6	3	1.6	106	14.5
Debit/credit cards	7	5.3	24	14.8	6	2.4	24	12.8	61	8.4
Money transfer	3	2.3	27	16.7	4	1.6	8	4.3	42	5.8
Health insurance	15	11.5	33	20.4	7	2.8	13	7.0	68	9.3
Life insurance	62	47.3	61	37.7	61	24.4	63	33.7	247	33.8
General insurance	58	44.3	16	9.9	17	6.8	23	12.3	114	15.6
Credit counseling	0	0	10	6.2	0	0	18	9.6	28	3.8
No access to any	8	6.1	18	11.1	7	2.8	63	33.7	96	13.2

Source: Field survey data.

Table 7.4

Sources of Information for Financial Inclusion

Source of Information	Nadimipalli (AP)		Kedinje (Karnataka)		Kayyar (Kerala)		Kundukulam (Tamil Nadu)		Total	
	No.	%	No.	%	No.	%	No.	%	No.	%
Family members/acquaintance	69	61.1	111	79.8	181	81.2	48	55.8	409	72.9
Advertisement/news	39	34.5	35	25.2	66	29.6	24	27.9	164	29.2
Bank employee/insurance agent	41	36.2	50	35.9	38	17.0	14	16.3	143	25.5
Government officials	34	30.1	10	7.2	8	3.6	9	10.5	61	10.9
NGO worker	19	16.8	4	2.9	8	3.6	6	6.9	37	6.6
SHG	57	50.4	24	17.3	21	9.4	42	48.8	144	25.7
Others	36	31.8	6	4.3	16	7.2	4	4.6	62	11.0

Note: Some respondents indicated more than one source of information. The percentages worked out based on the total households financially included/having access to financial services.

Source: Field survey data.

information for financial inclusion. In Kerala and Tamil Nadu villages, on the other hand, the households who have reported bank employee/ insurance agents are only 17 and 16 per cent respectively. As against this, in almost all the villages, family members/acquaintances are found to be the main source of information for financial inclusion. It is apparently clear that in dealing with the financial matters, the households in rural areas rely more on the advice of their family members or close acquaintances.

Other important sources of information mentioned are advertisement/ news articles and SHGs. Nearly 30 per cent of the financially included households in almost all selected villages have reported advertisement/ news or articles as their main source of information for financial inclusion. SHGs have also appeared to have played significant role in educating and motivating households for financial inclusion. In Andhra Pradesh and Tamil Nadu villages, nearly 50 per cent of the financially included households have reported SHGs as their main source of information. Surprisingly, in Karnataka and Kerala villages, 17 per cent and 9 per cent of the households respectively have reported SHGs as the main channel for financial inclusion. Except in Andhra village, in all other three villages, very few financially included households have reported government officials and NGOs as their source of information.

Since access essentially refers to the supply of financial services, it is therefore important to know which agencies the households prefer and have access for financial services. Since loan is a primary financial product supplied by the formal financial institutions, it is considered as proxy for finding out in the field survey the institutions to which the households have access. At the outset, it should be however, noted that the access of the households for loan facility depends on the proximity to the branch network of a particular agency. For example, in Kedinje village selected from Karnataka, Canara Bank has a branch and the regional rural bank has no branch nearby. The household response would naturally centre on Canara Bank branch. While interpreting the importance of various sources, this limitation of the data should be looked into. In Table 7.5, an attempt is made to analyse the responses of the households relating to the agencies from which, they have borrowed for their credit needs.

Table 7.5

Sources of Borrowing

Sources of Borrowings	Nadimipalli (AP)		Kedinje (Karnataka)		Kayyar (Kerala)		Kundukulam (Tamil Nadu)		Total	
	No.	%	No.	%	No.	%	No.	%	No.	%
Cooperative bank/society	13	11.5	30	21.6	11	4.9	6	7.0	60	10.7
Gramin bank	110	97.3	1	0.7	103	46.2	6	7.0	220	39.2
Commercial bank	37	32.7	63	45.3	57	25.6	25	29.1	182	32.4
Informal sources (Moneylenders)	75	66.4	8	5.7	12	5.4	47	54.6	142	25.3
Family members	31	27.4	15	10.8	11	4.9	17	19.8	74	13.2
Others	0	0.0	22	15.8	8	3.6	51	59.3	81	14.4

Note: Some household borrowed from more than one agency and hence percentages do not add to 100. Others refer to private finance companies etc.

Source: Field survey data.

From the table, it may be seen that though cooperatives have good network at village level, the households have more access to regional rural banks and commercial banks in all the villages studied. Surprisingly, informal agencies particularly moneylenders still play a dominant role in provision of loan facility in the villages studied in Andhra Pradesh and Tamil Nadu. Their role in the villages of Karnataka and Kerala appears to be only marginal. The main implication emerging from the analysis of the data is the importance of formal agencies like regional rural banks and commercial banks in providing financial services. Wherever they operate, households prefer to have access to them for their credit facilities.

Socioeconomic Profile of Financially Included

The study of socioeconomic status of the financially included and financially excluded is important not only to understand the dimensions of financial exclusion but also to know whether socioeconomic status acts as a barrier for expansion of financial inclusion. It is generally believed that social and economic characteristics of the potential customers have a large role in shaping or discouraging the access to financial services from formal financial institutions. A disaggregated analysis of financially included and excluded by gender, religion, caste, education level, occupation and household income is carried out based on the field data to determine the socioeconomic characteristics of those who are financially included and those who are financially excluded in different states. Instead of households, members of the households who are financially included are taken into consideration for the purpose as some of the households have more than one financially included. Table 7.6 presents the socioeconomic profile of financially included household members in different villages studied.

Table 7.6

Socioeconomic Profile of Financially Included

Indicators		Nadimipalli (AP)		Kedinje (Karnataka)		Kayyar (Kerala)		Kundukulam (Tamil Nadu)		Total	
		No.	%	No.	%	No.	%	No.	%	No.	%
Gender	Male	129	69.7	178	50.0	330	58.3	88	61.1	725	58.0
	Female	56	30.3	178	50.0	236	41.7	56	38.9	526	42.0
Religion	Hindu	182	98.4	288	80.9	290	51.2	144	100.0	904	72.3
	Christian	0	0	68	19.1	74	13.1	0	0	142	11.4
	Muslim	3	1.6	0	0	202	35.7	0	0	205	16.4
Caste	SC	3	1.6	23	6.5	32	5.7	21	14.6	79	6.3
	ST	4	2.2	20	5.6	8	1.4	0	0	32	2.6
	OBC	75	40.5	150	42.1	175	30.9	112	77.8	512	40.9
	Others	100	54.1	95	26.7	75	13.3	11	7.6	281	22.5
	Minority	3	1.6	68	19.1	276	48.8	0	0	347	27.7
Education level	SSLC plus	45	24.3	135	37.9	214	37.8	53	36.8	447	35.7
	Literate	41	22.2	83	23.3	164	29.0	39	27.1	327	26.1
	Semi-literate	37	20.0	58	16.3	86	15.2	17	11.8	198	15.8
	Illiterate	58	31.4	37	10.4	51	9.0	23	16.0	169	13.5
	Student	4	2.2	43	12.1	49	8.7	12	8.3	108	8.6
	Kid	0	0	0	0	2	0.4	0	0	2	0.2
Occupation	Agri-labour	56	30.3	35	9.8	42	7.4	22	15.3	155	12.4
	Non-agri. labour	7	3.8	60	16.9	184	32.5	36	25.0	287	22.9
	Artisans	0	0	5	1.4	9	1.6	4	2.8	18	1.4
	Petty business	2	1.1	31	8.7	32	5.7	5	3.5	70	5.6
	Farmer	101	54.6	8	2.2	7	1.2	9	6.3	125	10.0
	Others	11	5.9	120	33.7	111	19.6	37	25.7	279	22.3
	Housewife	2	1.1	25	7.0	95	16.8	16	11.1	138	11.0
	Student	4	2.2	10	2.8	49	8.7	12	8.3	75	6.0
	Not working	2	1.1	62	17.4	37	6.5	3	2.1	104	8.3

Source: Field survey data.

While the financially included households constitute slightly more than 80 per cent in the villages in Andhra Pradesh, Karnataka and Kerala, in Tamil Nadu, they constitute only 38 per cent of the bankable members of the households. The analysis of the field data on gender composition of household members financially included shows that in Andhra Pradesh and Tamil Nadu villages, gender differences in financial inclusion are very wide. Nearly two-thirds of the financially included in these villages are men and only one-third are women. As against this, in Karnataka and Kerala, the gender variations in financial inclusion are only marginal. While in Karnataka village, 50 per cent of the financially included are men and 50 per cent are women.

As regards religion, since the majority of the households studied belong to Hindu religion except in Kerala village, it is not possible to arrive at any conclusion on religion as a factor in promoting financial inclusion. In the Kerala village studied, the financially included belong to all religious groups on equal proportion to their population. The analysis of caste composition, on the other hand, shows that the majority of the financially included in Andhra Pradesh, Karnataka and Tamil Nadu villages belong to OBC and upper caste groups. In the Kerala village, minorities constitute nearly 50 per cent of the financially included. It is also important to note that a substantial number of SC and ST household members in Kerala and Karnataka villages are financially included.

The education level is a major factor in creating awareness and understanding of the financial products and services and thereby, in promoting financial inclusion. The analysis of data in Table 7.6 shows that in Karnataka, Kerala and Tamil Nadu villages, education level appears to play a dominant role in facilitating financial inclusion. Nearly 90 per cent of the financially included are literate and only 10 per cent belong to illiterate group. There is a positive correlation between the level of education and percentage of financially included. In Andhra village, on the other hand, no such pattern is observed. Nearly 31 per cent of the financially included are illiterate.

An understanding of occupation pattern of financially included is important as occupation plays a major role in determining entry to financial sector. Analysis of data in the table shows that since occupation pattern differs in different villages, it is difficult to generalise. In Andhra village, 55 per cent of the financially included belong to farming occupation and 30 per cent are agricultural labourers. Surprisingly, very few are non-agricultural labourers and having non-farm employment. Contrary to this in other villages, the majority of the financially included belong to non-farm employment and non-agricultural labourers. Financially included among farmers are found to be very few. Similarly, among homemakers financially included are very few except in Kerala village, where 17 per cent of them are home-makers. This may be mainly due to some family members working in the Gulf and channeling their remittance through the banking system. Surprisingly, in all the villages studied, a significant proportion of the financially included belong to agricultural labourers.

Since in the rural areas, it is difficult to compute accurately the income of individual members of the households, the field study focused on compilation of household income data only. In Table 7.7, an attempt is made to analyse the income of financially included households. The analysis reveals that income is an important determinant in financial inclusion. Only less than 5 per cent of the financially included households belong to an income level below Rs.10,000 per annum. Exception is observed in the case of the village studied in Kerala village, where nearly 19 per cent of the financially included have reported their household income below Rs.10,000.

In the villages selected in Andhra Pradesh, Karnataka and Tamil Nadu, more than 70 per cent of the financially included households have annual income of Rs.25,000 and above. Even in the case of Kerala village, the percentage of these households is 56. All these data collectively reveal that financially included belong to higher income groups.

Data relating to the assets position of the financially included households is analysed in Table 7.8, to explore whether the wealth of the households has any impact on financial inclusion.

Table 7.7

Income of Financially Included Households

Annual Income (Rupee)	Nadimipalli (AP)		Kedinje (Karnataka)		Kayyar (Kerala)		Kundukulam (Tamil Nadu)		Total	
	No.	%	No.	%	No.	%	No.	%	No.	%
Below 10000	2	1.8	2	1.4	43	19.3	5	5.8	52	9.3
10000-25000	26	23.0	19	13.7	54	24.2	19	22.1	118	21.0
25000-50000	33	29.2	32	23.0	72	32.3	26	30.2	163	29.1
50000-100000	33	29.2	37	26.6	36	16.1	22	25.6	128	22.8
100000 above	19	16.8	49	35.2	18	8.1	14	16.3	100	17.8
Total	113	100	139	100	223	100	86	100	561	100

Source: Field survey data.

Table 7.8

Asset Position of Financially Included Households

Assets	Nadimipalli (AP)		Kedinje (Karnataka)		Kayyar (Kerala)		Kundukulam (Tamil Nadu)		Total	
	No.	%	No.	%	No.	%	No.	%	No.	%
Land (hectare)										
None	1	0.9	85	61.2	119	53.4	58	67.4	263	46.9
Below 1.0	1	0.9	16	11.5	46	20.6	16	18.6	79	14.1
1.0–2.5	16	14.2	13	9.4	22	9.9	6	7.0	57	10.2
2.5–5.00	59	52.2	19	13.4	13	5.8	4	4.7	95	16.9
5.00 plus	36	31.9	6	4.4	23	10.3	2	2.3	67	11.9
Leased	0	0.0	0	0.0	0	0.0	0	0.0	0	0.0
House										
Owned	112	99.1	133	97.1	211	95.5	70	81.4	530	94.5
Leased	1	0.9	6	2.9	10	4.5	16	18.6	31	5.5
Cycle	30	26.5	30	21.6	18	8.1	58	67.4	136	24.2
Car	2	1.8	14	10.1	10	4.5	1	1.2	27	4.8
Motor cycle	43	38.1	33	23.7	36	16.1	31	36.0	143	25.5
Radio	30	26.5	78	56.1	117	52.5	40	46.5	265	47.2
TV	91	80.5	106	76.3	157	70.4	68	79.1	422	75.2
Gas stove	56	49.6	61	43.9	140	62.8	36	41.9	293	52.2
Telephone	47	41.6	70	50.4	155	69.5	8	9.3	280	49.9
Cellphone	69	61.1	107	77.0	151	67.7	63	73.3	390	69.5
Gold ornaments	98	86.7	120	86.3	212	95.1	58	67.4	488	87.0
Livestock	97	85.8	53	38.1	25	11.2	39	45.3	214	38.1
Electrification	112	99.1	127	91.4	211	94.6	80	93.0	530	94.5
Toilet	98	86.7	129	92.8	203	91.0	13	15.1	443	79.0

Source: Field survey data.

The ownership of assets facilitates easy access to financial services as banks usually look into the asset position of the clients and the collateral asset normally they require to lend. The ownership and size of the landholding is considered very important in rural areas in determining access to financial services from formal financial institutions. The analysis of data, however, reveals that except in the Andhra village, in all other three villages, the finding is contrary to this general belief. In the village studied in Andhra Pradesh, majority of the financially included households are medium and large farmers with land holding above 2.5 hectares. The number of financially included households among small and marginal farmers is negligible. As against this, in other three states, most of the financially included households are non-agriculturists without any landholding or are marginal farmers with less than one hectare. This may be due to non-farm occupation of non-agriculturists and the penetration made by SHG movement among landless and marginal farming community in these villages.

The analysis of data on other assets indicates that the financially included households belong to economically higher asset groups. Majority of the financially included households have their owned house, electrified, having latrine-toilet, gas stove, TV, cellphone and gold ornaments. Nearly one-fourth of the financially included households are found having cycles and motor cycles. In a nutshell, who you are and what is your economic status matter the most in financial inclusion.

Socioeconomic Profile of Financially Excluded

Out of 1690 bankable household members studied, 439 (26 per cent) are financially excluded. Tamil Nadu village has the highest number of financially excluded; out of 382 bankable members, 238 (62 per cent) are financially excluded. Kerala village has the lowest percentage (13) of financially excluded, followed by the village in Karnataka (17) and Andhra Pradesh (18). Table 7.9 provides the details of the socioeconomic characteristics of the financially excluded household members.

There are no wide differences in gender composition of financially excluded in all the four villages studied. Only in Karnataka and Tamil Nadu villages, the percentage of women in this category is more than men. The religion does not appear to be a factor in financial exclusion.

It is only in the Kerala sample, 57 per cent of the financially excluded belong to Muslim religion. As regards caste, in Andhra village, the majority of the financially excluded belong to OBC group. In Karnataka village, on the other hand, besides OBC, a significant proportion of the financially excluded belong to SC and upper caste groups. As against this, in Kerala, two-thirds of the financially excluded belong to minority group. In the Tamil Nadu village, 49 per cent of the financially excluded are of SCs and 47 per cent are OBC. Considering all the households studied, it is clear that the majority of the financially excluded (68 per cent) belong to SC and OBC caste groups.

The analysis of data relating to education levels reveals that in the villages in Andhra Pradesh, Karnataka and Tamil Nadu, more than 50 per cent of the financially excluded are either illiterates or semi-literates.

In the Kerala village, they constitute only 37 per cent of the financially excluded. With the higher level of education, the extent of financial exclusion was found lower. From the overall analysis of field data, it is apparently clear that education level plays a significant role in reducing financial exclusion. As regards occupation, the field data shows that majority of the financially excluded belong to agricultural labour and non-agricultural labour classes. The housewives also constitute 10 per cent of the total financially excluded. They constitute 18 per cent in the Kerala sample. The percentage of financially excluded belonging to farming community is only marginal. Surprisingly, in the villages from Andhra Pradesh and Kerala, a significant proportion of the financially excluded belong to non-agricultural workers.

Table 7.10 analyses the field data on household annual income of the financially excluded households. In all the villages studied, financially excluded belong to low income category of households. Nearly one-third of the financially excluded have annual household income below Rs.10,000. Another 40 per cent of them are in the income bracket of Rs.10000 and Rs.25000 per annum. Though the village in Kerala presents a slightly different picture, the overall trend is almost same. Only very few households belonging to higher income group are found to be financially excluded. They apparently belong to voluntarily excluded groups.

Details of the asset position of the financially excluded households in the villages selected are furnished in Table 7.11.

Table 7.9

Socioeconomic Profile of Financially Excluded

Indicators		Nadimipalli (AP)		Kedinje (Karnataka)		Kayyar (Kerala)		Kundukulam (Tamil Nadu)		Total	
		No.	%	No.	%	No.	%	No.	%	No.	%
Gender	Male	21	50.0	37	48.7	42	50.6	113	47.5	213	48.5
	Female	21	50.0	39	51.3	41	49.4	125	52.5	226	51.5
Religion	Hindu	42	100.0	73	96.1	27	32.5	238	100.0	380	86.6
	Christian	0	0	3	3.9	9	10.8	0	0	12	2.7
	Muslim	0	0	0	0	47	56.6	0	0	47	10.7
Caste	SC	0	0	15	19.7	0	0	116	48.7	131	29.8
	ST	0	0	2	2.6	0	0	3	1.3	5	1.1
	OBC	23	54.8	25	32.9	6	7.2	113	47.5	167	38.0
	Others	19	45.2	31	40.8	21	25.3	6	2.5	77	17.6
	Minority	0	0	3	3.9	56	67.5	0	0	59	13.4
Education level	SSLC plus	8	19.0	17	22.4	31	37.3	27	11.3	83	18.9
	Literate	6	14.3	19	25.0	21	25.3	55	23.1	101	23.0
	Semi-literate	7	16.7	18	23.7	18	21.7	47	19.7	90	20.5
	Illiterate	21	50.0	22	28.9	13	15.7	109	45.8	166	37.6
Occupation	Agri-labour	20	47.6	7	9.2	2	2.4	64	26.9	93	21.2
	Non-agri. labour	3	7.1	21	27.6	15	18.1	93	39.1	132	30.1
	Artisans	0	0	3	3.9	0	0	11	4.6	14	3.2
	Petty business	1	2.4	8	10.5	7	8.4	6	2.5	22	5.0
	Farmer	6	14.3	3	3.9	3	3.6	5	2.1	17	3.9
	Others	10	23.8	13	17.1	28	33.7	30	12.6	81	18.5
	Housewife	1	2.4	6	7.9	15	18.1	23	9.7	45	10.3
	Not working	1	2.4	15	19.7	13	15.7	6	2.5	35	8.0

Source: Field survey data.

Table 7.10

Household Income of Financially Excluded Households

Annual Income (Rupees)	Nadimipalli (AP)		Kedinje (Karnataka)		Kayyar (Kerala)		Kundukulam (Tamil Nadu)		Total	
	No.	%	No.	%	No.	%	No.	%	No.	%
Below 10000	6	33.3	7	30.4	9	33.3	26	25.7	48	28.4
10000-25000	8	44.4	9	39.1	7	25.9	41	40.6	65	38.5
25000-50000	3	16.7	4	17.4	6	22.3	23	22.8	36	21.3
50000-100000	0	0.0	2	8.7	4	14.8	6	5.9	12	7.1
1,00,000 above	1	5.6	1	4.4	1	3.7	5	5.0	8	4.7
Total	18	100	23	100	27	100	101	100	169	100

Source: Field survey data.

Table 7.11

Asset Position of Financially Excluded Households

Assets	Nadimipalli (AP)		Kedinje (Karnataka)		Kayyar (Kerala)		Kundukulam (Tamil Nadu)		Total	
	No.	%	No.	%	No.	%	No.	%	No.	%
Land (Ha)										
Owned: None	5	27.8	17	73.9	14	51.9	82	81.2	118	69.8
Below 1.0	0	0.0	3	13.0	6	22.2	13	12.9	22	13.0
1–2.5	4	22.2	1	4.3	3	11.1	6	5.9	14	8.3
2.5–5.00	8	44.4	2	8.7	1	3.7	0	0.0	11	6.5
5.00 plus	1	5.6	0	0.0	3	11.1	0	0.0	4	2.4
Leased	0	0.0	0	0.0	0	0.0	0	0.0	0	0.0
House										
Owned	16	88.9	22	95.7	26	96.3	80	79.2	144	85.2
Leased	2	11.1	1	4.3	1	3.7	21	20.8	25	14.8
Cycle	3	16.7	2	8.7	0	0.0	53	52.5	58	34.3
Car	0	0.0	0	0.0	0	0.0	1	1.0	1	0.6
Motor cycle	3	16.7	2	8.7	1	3.7	9	8.9	15	8.9
Radio	4	22.2	7	30.4	9	33.3	28	27.7	48	28.4
TV	10	55.6	12	52.2	15	55.6	63	62.4	100	59.2
Gas stove	4	22.2	3	13.0	13	48.1	8	7.9	28	16.6
Telephone	1	5.6	6	26.1	16	59.3	1	1.0	24	14.2
Cellphone	6	33.3	10	43.5	17	63.0	36	35.6	69	40.8
Jewellery	11	61.1	19	82.6	25	92.6	54	53.5	109	64.5
Livestock	11	61.1	9	39.1	4	14.8	36	35.6	60	35.5
Electrification	17	94.4	18	78.3	23	85.2	91	90.1	149	88.2
Toilet	10	55.6	20	87.0	23	85.2	2	2.0	55	32.5

Source: Field survey data.

In Karnataka, Kerala and Tamil Nadu villages, the financially excluded households are mostly found in the landless agricultural and non-agricultural labourer classes and marginal farmers. Among medium and large farming communities, the extent of financial exclusion is found to be only marginal. As against this, in Andhra village, financial exclusion is found more among small and medium farming communities. It is thus discernible that the proportion and level of inability to access financial services increases with the decline in size of landholding among farming community.

Most of the households in the villages studied in all the four states live in the owned houses. Hence, the ownership of the house may not be a decisive factor in financial exclusion. Notwithstanding this, in Tamil Nadu village, 20 per cent of the financially excluded households are found living in leased houses. As regards other assets, compared to financially included households, the proportion of financially excluded households having TV, cellphone, gas stove and other assets are significantly on the lower side. Evidently financial exclusion exists predominantly among the poor.

Reasons for Financial Exclusion

It is pertinent to examine as to why the households which need financial services have remained financially excluded and what are the reasons for the same. The reasons given by the households in fact reflect the main barriers for financial inclusion at the household level in rural areas. The field survey has therefore focused on compiling the perception of the financially excluded households regarding for financial inclusion. The findings of the field survey are analysed in Table 7.12.

The analysis of data provides an insight into the wide differences in the response pattern of the households with regard to the reasons for financial exclusion. In Andhra village, 50 per cent of the financially excluded households belong to voluntarily excluded category. They have indicated that they are not in need of banking services. In Karnataka village, their percentage is 43. In Tamil Nadu and Kerala villages, on the other hand, their percentages are significantly at lower levels. However, in the total households studied, the percentage of voluntary financial

Table 7.12

Reasons for Financial Exclusion

Reasons	Nadimipalli (AP)		Kedinje (Karnataka)		Kayyar (Kerala)		Kundukulam (Tamil Nadu)		Total	
	No.	%	No.	%	No.	%	No.	%	No.	%
Not aware of any bank	9	50.0	5	21.7	3	11.1	26	25.7	43	25.4
Bank is too far away	4	22.2	1	4.3	4	14.8	21	20.8	30	17.7
No security to offer	6	33.3	5	21.7	3	11.1	43	42.6	57	33.7
Fear of inability to repay	5	27.8	10	43.5	2	7.4	3	3.0	20	11.8
Too long to get loan	6	33.3	4	17.4	5	18.5	1	1.0	16	9.5
No need for banking services	9	50.0	10	43.5	8	29.6	17	16.8	44	26.0
Prefer to take loan from informal source	4	22.2	3	13.0	3	11.1	1	1.0	11	6.5
Not considered	6	33.3	5	21.7	0	0.0	13	12.9	24	14.2
Others	0	0.0	1	4.3	2	7.4	22	21.8	25	14.8

Note: Percentages are computed based on total financially excluded households. Multiple answers are allowed and hence percentages do not add upto 100.

Source: Field survey data.

exclusion is found to be, 26 per cent among the households not availing banking services.

As regards other reasons indicated, while in Andhra village, 50 per cent of the financially excluded households have reported that they are not aware of any bank branch nearby. In other villages, the households giving such reason are less than 25 per cent. A significant number of financially excluded households in Andhra Pradesh and Tamil Nadu villages also have indicated that bank is too far away as one of the reason for financial exclusion. Another important reason given in these two villages is their inability to offer required security. In Karnataka village, nearly 43 per cent of the financially excluded households have indicated an apprehension of their inability to repay as one of the important reason for financial exclusion. Another important finding of the study is that very few households in all the villages studied have indicated the ready availability of loan facility from informal sources as a reason for their disinterest in approaching financial institutions.

In order to probe further into the reasons for financial exclusion, in the field study, the households are asked: whether they are comfortable in going to the bank and if not, what are the reasons for their non-comfortability in accessing banks. There is a general perception that rural customers usually feel uncomfortable to approach bank because of its functional sophistication, technology, cumbersome procedure used and elite staff attitude. The customers' confidence and comfortability with financial institutions can have important influence on their willingness and preparedness to access such institutions. Any negative perception can have negative impact. The comfortability or ease of access is therefore considered very crucial on demand-side in motivating the customers in availing financial services rendered by the financial institutions. In Table 7.13, an attempt is made to evaluate the responses of all the households studied in this regard.

The majority of the households financially included in all the four villages studied have reported that they are very much comfortable with the bank. In Andhra village, almost all 113 financially included households are found to be comfortable with the bank. In other villages, some of the financially included households have reported non-comfortability with the bank, though their number is very few. As

Table 7.13

Comfortability in Going to the Bank

Indicators	Nadimipalli (AP)		Kedinje (Karnataka)		Kayyar (Kerala)		Kundukulam (Tamil Nadu)		Total	
	No.	%	No.	%	No.	%	No.	%	No.	%
Comfortable	113	86.3	134	82.7	213	85.2	76	40.6	536	73.4
Not comfortable	18	13.7	28	17.3	37	14.8	111	59.4	194	26.6
Total	131	100	162	100	250	100	187	100	730	100
Reasons for non-comfortable										
Too far from home	1	5.5	5	17.8	0	0	39	35.1	45	23.2
No bus service	0	0	13	46.4	0	0	21	18.9	34	17.5
Unfriendly attitude of bank staff	6	33.3	15	53.6	8	21.6	17	15.3	46	23.7
High interest rates	11	61.1	11	39.3	16	43.2	21	18.9	59	30.4
Lack of information	13	72.2	14	77.8	14	37.8	27	24.3	68	35.0
Lack of trust in the unknown bank	4	22.2	15	53.6	1	2.7	16	14.4	36	18.5
Fear of technology used by the bank	10	55.5	9	32.1	1	2.7	18	16.2	38	19.6
Ready available local moneylender	10	55.5	11	39.3	0	0	15	13.5	36	18.5
Bank has never approached	8	44.4	19	67.8	10	27.0	27	24.3	64	32.9

Source: Field survey data.

expected, all the financially excluded households have indicated non-comfortability in accessing the banks.

Regarding the reasons for non-comfortability in accessing banks, it may be seen from the table that the there is no uniform pattern of response in all the villages studied. In Andhra Pradesh village lack of information, high interest rate, fear of technology used by the bank and readily available loans from local moneylender are reported as the main reasons for non-comfortability in going to the bank.

In Karnataka village, on the other hand, lack of information, "bank never approached", unfriendly attitude of the bank staff, and lack of trust in the unknown bank are mentioned as the main reasons for non-comfortability. High interest rate, fear of bank technology and availability of informal finance are not reported as reasons for non-comfortability. In Kerala village, high interest rate and lack of information appear to be the main reasons for non-comfortability in accessing bank. In Tamil Nadu village, the responses of the households widely differ, though higher percentage of households have indicated geographical distance, lack of information and absence of approach by the bank as the main reasons for non-comfortability in accessing banks.

SHGs as Strategic Tool for Financial Inclusion

As already indicated in the earlier chapter, the SHGs are considered as the most appropriate and potent initiative for reaching the unreached and for delivering financial services to the poor and vulnerable section of the community in a sustainable manner. With a view to ascertain whether SHGs can be used as strategic tool for financial inclusion, the data are compiled in the field study on membership of the SHGs in relation to financial inclusion. The findings are presented in Table 7.14.

The analysis of data confirms that there is a close correlation between the financial inclusion and membership of SHGs. In Andhra Pradesh, Karnataka and Kerala villages, all SHG member households are financially included. In Tamil Nadu village, however, the number of SHG member households exceeds financially included households. Out of 108 SHG member households, 22 households are found to be financially excluded. The possible reason for this may be: either they are newly formed and yet to link with the banks or they solely depend on sponsoring NGOs for their financial services.

Table 7.14

SHG Members among Financially Included Households

State	Respondents (Number)	Financially Included (Number)	Members of SHG (Number)	Per cent of SHG Members	
				In Total Households	In Financially Included
Nadimipalli (Andhra Pradesh)	131	113	83	63.36	73.45
Kedinje (Karnataka)	162	139	45	27.78	32.37
Kayyar (Kerala)	250	223	45	18.00	20.18
Kundukulam (Tamil Nadu)	187	86	108	57.75	100.00*
Total	730	561	281	38.49	50.08

Note: * In Tamil Nadu, the SHG members were more than financially included.

Source: Field survey data.

Notwithstanding this, the SHG-bank linkage has played major role in financial inclusion in the selected villages of Andhra Pradesh and Tamil Nadu. In Andhra village, 73 per cent of the financially included are SHG members. In Tamil Nadu village, almost 100 per cent of the financially included are SHG member households. In Karnataka and Kerala villages, more than SHGs, other factors have played a role in financial inclusion. In Kerala village, hardly 20 per cent of financially included households are SHG members and the balance 80 per cent are not SHG members. Similarly in Karnataka village, the percentage of SHG members in the total households studied is relatively very low (28 per cent). However, the field study empirically demonstrates that SHGs are the strategic agency for promotion of financial inclusion at household level in rural areas in all the villages studied.

Support Needed for Financial Inclusion

It is important to know the perception of the potential customers on the support needed for financial inclusion from financial institutions, particularly banks. There is a latent demand for financial products and services and financial institutions require unlocking the demand or stimulating it by providing the required support by "look through the eyes of their potential customers". Hence, in the field study, the respondents are asked to identify the support required for improving their access to financial services from formal financial institutions. The findings are presented in Table 7.15.

From the table, it may be seen that the pattern of responses received is almost similar in all the villages studied. The majority of the respondents have indicated that they need information about the bank and also help in using the bank services. This implies that most of the respondents are not well-acquainted with the functioning of the various financial agencies and how to avail the benefit of the services rendered by them. Unless there is a substantial degree of trust and confidence in the functioning of institutions, they will not come forward to avail banking facilities. Hence, they are badly in need of financial literacy campaigns for providing information, sensitisation and training. Unless this is done, they cannot develop confidence and trust with the institutions.

Other important support elements identified are advice on investing savings and advice on procuring farm inputs, and advice on modern farm practices. These support elements mainly centred around face-to-face financial counseling and advisory services in how to use productively the financial services rendered by them. This will improve the absorptive capacity of the excluded segments. Thus, the analysis of the field data on support needed demonstrates that financial literacy campaign, financial counseling and advisory services are most critical elements for promoting financial inclusion and augmenting demand for financial products and services in rural India.

Determinants of Financial Inclusion

As already defined, financial inclusion refers to access to a range of financial products and services, which include saving schemes, loans, insurance, money transfer and remittance, mutual fund etc. In this section, an attempt is made to construct financial inclusion index based

Table 7.15

Support Needed from the Bank to Improve Financial Inclusion

Support Elements	Nadimipalli (AP)		Kedinje (Karnataka)		Kayyar (Kerala)		Kundukulam (Tamil Nadu)		Total	
	No.	%	No.	%	No.	%	No.	%	No.	%
Information about the bank	81	61.8	92	56.8	180	72.0	124	66.3	477	65.3
Help in using bank services	91	69.5	80	49.4	154	61.6	105	56.1	430	58.9
Guidance in procuring farm inputs	58	44.3	34	20.9	30	12.0	33	17.6	155	21.2
Advice on modern farm practices	46	35.1	36	22.2	27	10.8	34	18.2	143	19.6
Advice on investing savings	72	55.0	75	46.3	111	44.4	84	44.9	342	46.8

Source: Field survey data.

on the extent of use of these products and services by the individual households in different villages studied and determine the factors associated with the level of financial inclusion. The index of financial inclusion is a broad measure of inclusiveness in access/use of financial products and services. It is constructed as multidimensional index that captures information on access and usage of various financial products offered by the financial system at the household level.

The financial products and services selected for construction of financial inclusion index are savings account, loan account, Kisan Credit Card, mutual fund, life insurance, health/general insurance and money transfer and remittance. For measurement of various financial products and services, financial exclusion is given value of 0 and inclusion is measured based on scores with weights assigned, based on their importance. Since access/use of saving and loan facilities is more important in discussion of financial inclusion at the present juncture, they are given a maximum score of 25 each. Other products are given the maximum score of 10 each.[1] Scores are assigned proportionately depending on number of household members having availed the various financial products and services. The index is constructed for each household based on the minimum score of 0 for financial exclusion and maximum score of 100 for financial inclusiveness of all selected financial products and services. Thus, the financial inclusion index measures broadly the level of financial inclusion of households studied in different villages.

The distribution of the households based on the financial inclusion index in different villages is given in Table 7.16.

The analysis of the data shows that in Tamil Nadu village, 43 per cent of the households studied are financially excluded with zero value. In other villages, the financially excluded households are only about 6 per cent of the households studied. This implies that financial exclusion is very high in the village studied in Tamil Nadu. While in other states, most of the financially included households are in the

---

1. Scores are assigned arbitrarily. In rural areas, more emphasis on financial inclusion studies is given to improving access to saving and loan facilities, these variables are given higher weights. Other variables of financial inclusion are considered of equal importance for assigning weights.

Table 7.16

Distribution of Households based on Financial Inclusion Index

Index	Nadimipalli (AP)		Kedinje (Karnataka)		Kayyar (Kerala)		Kundukulam (Tamil Nadu)		Total	
	No.	Per cent	No.	Per cent	No.	Per cent	No.	Per cent	No.	Per cent
0	8	6.1	11	6.8	14	5.6	80	42.8	113	15.5
1-10	0	0.0	2	1.2	0	0.0	2	1.1	4	0.5
10-20	4	3.0	32	19.7	64	25.6	34	18.2	134	18.4
20-30	1	0.8	22	13.6	36	14.4	27	14.4	86	11.8
30-40	9	6.9	32	19.7	50	20.0	17	9.1	108	14.8
40-50	39	29.8	28	17.4	39	15.6	19	10.2	125	17.1
50-60	43	32.8	27	16.7	34	13.6	4	2.1	108	14.8
60-70	27	20.6	7	4.3	11	4.4	3	1.6	48	6.6
70-80	0	0.0	1	0.6	2	0.8	1	0.5	4	0.5
80-90	0	0.0	0	0.0	0	0.0	0	0.0	0	0.0
90-100	0	0.0	0	0.0	0	0.0	0	0.0	0	0.0
Total	131	100.0	162	100.0	250	100.0	187	100.0	730	100.0

Note: Index 0 reflects financial exclusion in all financial products/services. In the earlier tables, financially excluded refer to those who have no bank accounts (saving or loan).

Source: Field survey data.

index range between 30 and 60, in Tamil Nadu, they are in the range between 10 and 30. Hardly 7 households out of 187 households studied are found with financial index above 50. The pattern of distribution of households based on financial inclusion index is more or less similar in Karnataka and Kerala villages. In Andhra village, nearly 53 per cent of the households are found with financial inclusion index above 50. This is not the feature found in other villages.

The factors that affect financial inclusion are several and their interactions with each other are very complex. Without going into the complexity of various factors determining the level of financial inclusion at the household level, an attempt is made by using correlation matrix and regression model to identify the factors that are associated with some degree of significance, to the index of financial inclusion. The financial inclusion index is considered as dependent variable and causal factors as independent variables considered are: social status, education, housing condition, SHG membership, income and landholding as proxy for asset position of the households.[2] It should be noted at the outset that the causal factors selected for correlation and regression analysis are mainly on demand-side only. Supply-side factors which are also critical for determining financial inclusion at the household level are not considered. The correlation and regression coefficients are computed for each village studied separately.

The correlation coefficients of various independent variables with financial inclusion index computed for households in different villages are shown in Table 7.17.

---

2.   Social status is measured by scoring based caste status; education by education level; housing measured by assigning score based on whether owned or leased; SHG members by assigning scores based on number of memberships in the households; income based on annual income of the households; and land based on size of landholdings.

Table 7.17

*Correlation Coefficients of Important Determinants
of Financial Inclusion*

Variables	Nadimipalli (AP)	Kedinje (Karnataka)	Kayyar (Kerala)	Kundukulam (Tamil Nadu)
Social status	0.118	0.105	0.087	0.253**
Education	0.245**	0.326**	0.252**	0.519**
Housing condition	0.324**	-0.087	0.022	0.179*
SHG membership	0.225**	0.110	0.054	0.237**
Household income	0.320**	0.332**	0.143**	0.371**
Landholding	0.371**	0.207*	-0.038	0.274**

Note: * Significant at 5 per cent level, ** Significant at 1 per cent level.

Source: Field survey data.

The analysis of correlation coefficients shows that the most important variables significantly and positively correlated with the financial inclusion index are education level and household income followed by SHG memberships. Surprisingly, social status has not found significantly correlated with financial index except in Tamil Nadu village. In Andhra village, more than education, house ownership, household income and landholding have higher correlation coefficients with the financial inclusion index. The social status has the lowest correlation coefficient. In Karnataka village, on the other hand, household income and education have the higher correlation coefficients followed by landholding. Social status and SHG membership have lower correlation with financial inclusion. House ownership has, in fact, negative correlation with financial inclusion.

In Kerala village, the main factor determining financial inclusion appears to be education level and household income. Landholding has negative correlation implying thereby more financial exclusion among large landholding farming community. Tamil Nadu village, however, presents a different picture. All six factors selected have positive and significantly higher influence on financial inclusion. Education has the positive correlation coefficient of 0.519 followed by household income (0.371). Among the villages studied, Tamil Nadu village has the highest correlation coefficients for social status, SHG membership and land-holding.

The multiple regression models are constructed for each village studied separately to determine the relative importance of the various determinants of the financial inclusion. Financial inclusion index is considered as dependent variable (Y) and social status (X_1), education level (X_2), household income (X_3), landholding (X_4), housing conditions (X_5) and SHG membership (X_6) as independent variables. Table 7.18 contains the estimates of the regression analysis carried out.

Table 7.18

Regression Estimates of Determinants of Financial Inclusion

Determinants	Nadimipalli (AP)		Kedinje (Karnataka)		Kayyar (Kerala)		Kundukulam (Tamil Nadu)	
	Coefficient	Std. Error	Coefficient	Std. Error	Coefficient	Std. Error	Coefficient	Std. Error
Constant	2.692	0.659	3.692	0.682	3.113	0.676	-0.268	0.471
X_1	0.008	0.055	0.038	0.062	-0.006	0.058	0.125	0.081
X_2	0.063	0.040	0.129	0.042	0.142	0.032	0.204	0.034
X_3	0.166	0.129	0.112	0.112	0.351	0.087	0.379	0.099
X_4	0.148	0.070	-0.039	0.060	0.121	0.058	0.148	0.080
X_5	0.129	0.059	-0.044	0.063	-0.048	0.049	0.015	0.33
X_6	0.202	0.059	0.076	0.056	0.090	0.042	0.168	0.047
R^2		0.518		0.088		0.212		0.396

Note: * Significant at 5 per cent level, ** Significant at 1 per cent level.
Source: Field survey data.

The regression analysis shows that the relative importance of the six selected variables differs in their influence in determining the extent of financial inclusion in different villages. In Andhra village, membership of SHG followed by household income, landholding and housing condition are found to be important determinants of financial inclusion index. The education level and social status are not found to be important. The R^2 at 0.518 indicates that all these variables collectively explain 52 per cent of the variations in financial inclusion. Considering the fact that the supply-side factors are not taken into account, the resultant R^2 is found to be quite significant. Contrary to this, in the case of the village studied in Karnataka, all these variables explain only 9 per cent of the variation in the financial inclusion index. Among the variables selected, only education level and household income are found to have significant positive influence on financial inclusion in this village.

In the Kerala village, household income followed by education level and landholding are found to be important determinants of financial inclusion. The social status and housing condition have, surprisingly, negative influence on financial inclusion. As against this, in Tamil Nadu village, except landholding all other variables are found to be important determinants of financial inclusion.

8 | Financial Inclusion
The Road Traversed So Far

The concept of financial inclusion has become the most widely used objective in all the literatures and annual reports of the banks in India ever since the Governor of the Reserve Bank of India emphasised the need for extending banking facilities to all the unreached households. Recognising the regional inequalities in the availability of banking facilities, it was thought expedient to cover within a short time span at least one district in each state, by achieving 100 per cent financial inclusion. During the last four years, some efforts were made by the banks to reach out to people of all strata to enrol them as bank customers. Much publicity was given to this achievement. All the annual reports of banks, particularly of the public sector banks, have made special reference to their achievements in this task. In this chapter, a review of the achievements made by banks as on March 2009 is made first. Analysing the implications thereof an action plan for going beyond financial inclusion is drawn.

RBI's Annual Policy Statement for the Year 2009-10

The Reserve Bank of India making a review of the action initiated by the banking sector till date in its Annual Policy Statement for the year 2009-2010, states, "So far, 344 districts have been identified by SLBCs for 100 per cent financial inclusion. Of these, 175 districts in 21 States and 7 Union Territories have reported having achieved the target. All districts of Haryana, Himachal Pradesh, Karnataka, Kerala, Uttarakhand, Goa, Chandigarh, Puducherry, Daman and Diu, Dadra and Nagar Haveli and Lakshadweep have reported having achieved 100 per cent financial inclusion" (Reserve Bank of India, 2009). It is also mentioned that, "Banks were advised in January 2009, among other things:

(i)   "To ensure provision of banking services nearer to the location of the no-frills account holders through a variety of channels.

(ii)   "To provide General Credit Card (GCC)/small overdrafts along with no-frills accounts to encourage the account holders to actively operate the accounts.

(iii) "To conduct awareness drives so that the no-frills account holders were made aware of the facilities offered.

(iv)   "To review the extent of coverage in districts declared as 100 per cent financially included, and

(v)   "To efficiently leverage on the technology enabled financial inclusion solutions currently available."

The expectation of the regulator is that the banks should do much more than padding their bulky ledger books with the mere number of new savings bank accounts. However, the published annual reports of banks do not provide adequate details of the actions taken by them in all the above mentioned aspects. The disclosures made in the Directors' Annual Report of FY2009 of some of the south-based public sector banks are quoted below.

Review of the Actions Taken

From the available data, it appears that most of the banks have vigorously pursued the opening of no-frills accounts rather than making visible progress in other action points. Some banks have taken the initiative of expanding their branch network, while a few have adopted the branchless banking model for reaching out to new customers. The achievement made so far in this area is very insignificant in terms of numbers. But it has opened a new vista for enhancing rural reach of banks through a cost-effective mode, using very simple IT-based operations utilising the services of business correspondents. It has immense potentialities in making financial inclusion a reality. The progress made by banks in the above five directions is briefly presented below.

Inadequacies of Banking Spread

Branch expansion programme of the banking sector has not been made an integral part of the efforts for attaining financial inclusion. Since the implementation of financial sector reforms, rural banking has lost the priority and there has been a deceleration of rural branch expansion since 1992. The Reserve Bank of India in its branch licensing policy has not laid special emphasis on rural branch expansion, with a view to accelerate the process of financial inclusion.

After the announcement of the targets for financial inclusion, the banking sector has witnessed the opening of 9,585 new branches from March 2006 to March 2009. Out of them, only 910 are rural branches, taking their total number from 30,579 to 31,489. Out of them, *gramin* banks account for nearly 30 per cent of the new rural branches (316) opened. During the same period, the number of urban and metropolitan branches opened by commercial banks has gone up by 5,467 new branches. Over 80 districts were identified as poorly banked districts, where the regional rural banks are not operating. The union territory of Puducherry was one of the identified areas, where a regional rural bank—Puduvai Bharathiar Grama Bank—was established in June 2008 (Thingalaya, 2008). About the other districts, details are not available relating to the new rural branches opened.

Opening of a new rural branch contributes more to the process of financial inclusion by providing proximity to banking facilities than the opening of an urban branch. In the latter case, it would more likely to be sharing of the existing customers of other banks operating in the area. In an unbanked rural area, a new branch would be invariably resulting in bringing to the banking fold new customers. This aspect does not appear to have received official recognition in the policy framework of branch expansion amenable to financial inclusion. No doubt, financial inclusion initiatives have to be undertaken in the cities also. However, since the banking penetration ratio is dismally poor in rural areas in most of the states, for mitigating this imbalance, more rural branches need to be opened, particularly in the backward states.

Issuing General Credit Cards

This being a continuation of an existing programme, banks are expected to increase the number of such cards issued during the last four years. The RBI's Annual Policy Statement, however, does not provide any clue about the extent to which this facility has been utilised by the borrowers.

Canara Bank reports that "As a measure of taking the financial products to the excluded, the Bank has sanctioned 1,24,732 General Credit Cards (GCC) since inception and the total exposure under GCC as at March 2009 stood at Rs.217 crore."

Syndicate Bank has issued 10,314 syndicate general credit cards with an outlay of Rs.22.69 crore as on March 2009.

Corporation Bank makes a passing reference stating that "The Bank has opened more than 4.5 lakh no-frills saving bank accounts and has issued more than 19,000 General Credit Cards."

Indian Bank indicates that "Covering 4637 villages, the Bank under the Financial Inclusion Project, opened 17.04 lakh No Frills SB accounts and provided Overdraft and GCC facilities to 52,545 individuals with a total sum of Rs.10.91 crore."

Indian Overseas Bank also makes a passing reference stating that it has issued 19,934 general credit cards during the year FY 2009.

Vijaya Bank merely reports, "The Bank took forward the initiative in the second phase of the programme by extending Vijaya General Credit Cards and other need based facilities to the beneficiaries covered under the first phase."

Besides the general credit cards, the public sector banks have been issuing Kisan Credit Cards since 1999 to facilitate the borrowings of farmers. The total number of such cards issued so far is 3.51 crore and the amount of credit outstanding is Rs.1,77,607 crore. To what extent the general credit cards have been issued by banks as a part of their plans for financial inclusion in their lead districts cannot be assessed from the modicum details available. While no-frills accounts get a pride of place in the banks' efforts to enhance financial inclusion, these cards fail to get more attention.

Conducting Awareness Drives

Banks which have developed a proactive apparatus for discharging the lead bank responsibilities over the years, have been active in creating awareness about the facilities available besides the no-frills accounts. All banks are not very prompt in publishing the progress made by them in this regard.

Canara Bank has mentioned in its Annual Report that "In a novel initiative, the Bank has launched Gramin Vikas Vahini-vehicles to spread *financial literacy*. Under this initiative, 50 vans were operational in 50 districts across India. The Bank has started Credit Counselling Centres in three districts in Karnataka to enhance financial literacy."

Syndicate Bank in association with the *gramin* banks sponsored by it "has set up Financial Literacy-cum Counselling centres in 8 centres in Bijapur and Chikodi in Karnataka, Kadapa in Andhra Pradesh, Rewari in Haryana, J.P. Nagar, Moradabad and Rampur in Uttar Pradesh and Kannur in Kerala."

Vijaya Bank merely mentions, "Counselling centres under financial literacy programmes were also opened at select centres during the year."

Indian Bank "has opened 20 banking service centres to provide doorstep banking for the rural masses."

The Reserve Bank of India has indicated in the Annual Statement its dissatisfaction about the tardy progress made by banks in this area: "So far, banks have reported setting up or proposing to set up 123 credit counselling centres in various States of the country. The feedback received in this regard indicated that most of these centres were in effect set up as extensions of the bank branches and engaged in promotion of banks specific products. Accordingly, a model scheme on financial literacy and credit counselling centres (FLCCs) was formulated and communicated to all scheduled commercial banks and RRBs with the advice to set up the centres as distinct entities maintaining an arm's length from the bank, so that the FLCC's services are available to even other banks' customers in the district." The achievements of banks in adhering to these guidelines are yet to be known.

Leveraging Technology-enabled Solution

One of the notable innovations made by banks in leveraging technology-enabled solution for financial inclusion is the adoption of branchless banking mode, particularly in the rural areas. Appointing a business correspondent in a village and distributing smart cards to the villagers interested in dealing with the bank, banking transactions are made in the village itself without opening a brick and mortar branch. A small IT-based gadget, Integra is used to facilitate and record the banking transactions like depositing and withdrawing money. The smart card-holder is relieved from the trouble of travelling to the branch situated away from his village and also from incurring the expenditure for travelling. This little saving of the bus fare also could be deposited to his account at the business correspondent's house, which works as the virtual branch (Thingalaya, 2007).

Corporation Bank was the first public sector bank to introduce branchless banking. A beginning was made in Dakshina Kannada district in 2006. "The Bank has 411 business correspondents as on March 31-3-2009 spread over all southern states and they collectively clock nearly 10,000 transactions a month", its Annual Report reveals.

Syndicate Bank reports, "Branchless banking/Smart card project through Business Correspondents is taken up on a pilot basis in our lead districts of Bellary in Karnataka, Anantapur and Kurnool in Andhra Pradesh in collaboration with respective state governments for payment of wages under NREGP/SSP."

Canara Bank, without disclosing details, mentions that "The Bank took several technology initiatives to further financial inclusion process like multi-lingual bio-metric ATMs, voice-enabled mobile bio-metric ATM and launching Smart Card project."

Indian Overseas Bank explains, "Smart card banking with the use of biometric smartcards and handheld devices to facilitate banking transactions at the doorsteps of villagers has been introduced at Kuttam Bakkam (Tiruvallur District) and Kameshwaram (Nagapattinam District which was earlier devastated by tsunami). The devices are voice-enabled in vernacular language and user-friendly for illiterates. 1173 biometric smart cards have been issued under review."

Vijaya Bank announces, "With a view to providing banking facilities at the door step of the beneficiaries covered under the financial inclusion programme, the Bank introduced Vijaya Vikas Smart Cards, an

IT-enabled financial inclusion initiative through business correspondent model on a pilot basis in 7 villages of Mandya district, Karnataka."

This innovation is in its nascent stage, confined to a few villages in some states. Full details of its operations are not available in any published sources, except what is disclosed in the Directors' Reports of the banks concerned, as quoted above. This model would be very useful in reaching out to the unreached, if adopted by all banks in a planned manner. It is quite reassuring to note that the Government of India is keen to route its wage disbursals to the participants in the National Rural Employment Guarantee Programme (NREGP) through bank accounts in the villages. In facilitating this process, the branchless model would be an ideal arrangement.

Reviewing the Extent of Coverage

Banks continue to make their claims of achieving 100 per cent financial inclusion in most of their lead districts. In the past, many state electricity boards have taken pride in announcing total rural electrification, when the electricity power lines pass through the villages. If one household in the village is electrified, it cannot be said that the whole village is electrified and rural electrification is achieved 100 per cent. What could not be achieved in 60 years of planning cannot be achieved overnight. Similarly, if one person in each household in a district opens a no-frills account, it is not prudent to conclude that all households are covered under financial inclusion. Whatever claims the major south-based banks have made in their Annual Reports are quoted below:

Canara Bank: "The Bank achieved Total Financial Inclusion in all the 25 lead districts spread over five states namely, Karnataka, Kerala, Tamil Nadu, Bihar, Uttar Pradesh. The state of Kerala, where Canara Bank is the convenor of State Level Bankers' Committee, was the first major state to achieve total financial inclusion in the year 2007. The Bank mobilised 5.62 lakhs no frills accounts (*CanSaral*) during 2008-09 and reached a cumulative level of 17.29 lakhs since inception. The total savings in the no-frills accounts reached a level of Rs.276 crore in 16,57,749 accounts" (Canara Bank, 2009).

Syndicate Bank: "The Bank has achieved 100 per cent financial inclusion in all its 25 lead districts in 5 states and one union territory for extending all types of banking services. For the Bank as a whole, 34.56 lakh no-frills accounts were opened under financial inclusion in the country as on 31ˢᵗ March 2009" (Syndicate Bank, 2009).

Vijaya Bank: "After successfully completing the first phase of financial inclusion, the Bank took forward the initiative in the second phase of the programme by extending Vijaya General Credit Cards and other need-based credit facilities to the beneficiaries covered under the first phase" (Vijaya Bank, 2009).

Corporation Bank is one bank perhaps, which has not claimed to have achieved 100 per cent financial inclusion in any district. But it has made remarkable progress in this direction, as disclosed in its Annual Report. It said, "The Bank has started financial inclusion way back in July 2006. The Bank has conducted village surveys in 1332 villages in the states of Karnataka, Andhra Pradesh, Tamil Nadu, Kerala, Goa, Maharashtra, West Bengal and Madhya Pradesh which enables the branches to draw a household business model and a village credit plan consolidating all credit needs of the identified village" (Corporation Bank, 2009).

Indian Bank: "Besides achieving total financial inclusion (involving all Banks) in UT of Puducherry, Cuddalore (Tamil Nadu) and Kollam (Kerala), the Bank has implemented 100 per cent Financial Inclusion in 9 other lead districts. 100 per cent Financial Inclusion has also been completed by the Bank in Nilgiris (ST concentrated), Tiruvarur (SC concentrated) and Kaniyakumari (minorities concentrated) districts". (Indian Bank, 2009).

Indian Overseas Bank: "In order to bring hitherto excluded people under banking fold, the bank has opened 7,28,894 no frills S.B accounts and granted 19,934 general purpose credit cards" (Indian Overseas Bank, 2009).

Andhra Bank is reported to have achieved 100 per cent financial inclusion in Ganjam district of Orissa and Srikakulam district of Andhra Pradesh.

State Bank of Hyderabad: "Districts of Nizamabad and Ranga Reddy in A.P. and Koppal and Raichur in Karnataka where the Bank has lead bank responsibilities have achieved 100 per cent financial inclusion" (State Bank of Hyderabad, 2009).

State Bank of Travancore: "As a part of Financial Inclusion, the Bank has opened 7,92,385 'Janapriya' No-frills accounts with an outstanding of Rs.125.77crore as on 31ˢᵗ March 2009, of which 2,02,660 accounts were opened during the year. In Kerala State we have a market share of 72.4 per cent of the amount outstanding under No-frills accounts. As a second stage of Financial Inclusion, we have taken various initiatives on Financial Education/Financial Literacy and Credit Counseling. This includes sanctioning of General Purpose Credit Cards (GCC) to the eligible and the needy, strengthening Self Help Group lending, finance to tenant farmers and share croppers and issue of insurance products" (State Bank of Travancore, 2009).

One of the grey areas in achieving total financial inclusion, which is often ignored, is the coverage of the migrant population in the cities. In every city there are large groups of migrant labourers, working in construction activities and females working as housemaids. They are usually not inducted into banking, because of the requirements under the know your customer (KYC) guidelines. These people are not necessarily those below the poverty line. They have reasonably good income and need small doses of credit and also the facility for money transfer. But they cannot approach the banks as they do not have permanent residence. They remain excluded in the cities where they work and they are not included in their villages, as they have migrated to towns. Total financial inclusion under such circumstances appears to be elusive.

Latest Initiatives: An Overdose?

For hastening the process of financial inclusion, the Reserve Bank of India has been propagating the adoption of business correspondent model as recommended by Report of the Internal Group to Examine Issues Relating to Rural Credit and Microfinance (Reserve Bank of India, 2005). It has recommended outsourcing the services of retired bank employees, among many others, for conducting some transactions. The branchless banking model, where the business correspondents manage the virtual branch is based on this model. With the blessing of the regulator, some banks have already started using this model for reaching out to new customers in a limited manner.

For carrying this process further, the Reserve Bank of India has appointed a working group to review the business correspondent model and to recommend action programmes for using this model as an important part of the financial inclusion strategy. The working group has submitted its report on August 18, 2009, which is made available on the website of Reserve Bank of India from August 19, 2009. The major recommendations pertain to enlarging the number of players at the grassroot level with a view to ensure that the process of financial inclusion gains further momentum (Reserve Bank of India, 2009).

"The Working Group has recommended the following new entities for appointment of Business Correspondents for banks in rural and semi-urban areas:

"i) Individual kirana/medical/fair price shop owners, ii) Individual Public Call Office (PCO) operators, iii) Agents of Small Savings Schemes of Government of India/Insurance Companies, iv) Individuals who own petrol pumps, v) Retired teachers, vi) Authorised functionaries of well run Self Help Groups (SHGs) linked to banks, vii) Non deposit taking NBFCs (non-banking finance companies) in the nature of loan companies whose micro finance portfolio is not less than 80 per cent of their loan outstanding in the financially excluded districts as identified by the Committee on Financial Inclusion (Chairman: Dr. C. Rangarajan)."

The other major recommendation of the working group include measures for improving the long-term viability of the BC model by permitting banks to collect reasonable service charges from the customer in a transparent manner for delivering the services through the BC and handholding of BCs by banks in the initial stages.

A wide variety of people from shopkeepers, PCO operators, petrol pump owners, small saving agents, retired teachers to the coordinators of SHGs can be roped in by banks to work as business correspondents.

Retired bank employees are already included in this list. While the intention is very genuine, the induction of a large number of persons drawn from these diverse fields is likely to create problems of supervision and control. Where cash is involved, specially scattered in the hands of persons of different backgrounds in a large number of villages, misuse of funds may emerge as a major problem. Supervision of these BCs would add to the cost of operations. A cautious approach drafting initially the services of retired bank staff specially from the *gramin* banks may be more expedient.

It may be recalled that the earlier Report has cautioned about the risks involved by stating, "The experience of banks most of the time has been adverse, with cash leakage, frauds and accounting and reconciliation problems. Most of the banks have now closed such schemes after booking losses." However, recognising the intrinsic advantages of the business correspondence model, the same Report has rightly indicated, "There is need to learn from this experience and device adequate checks and balances and utilize IT tools to make any future initiatives less risky for banks."

It is reported that the total number of business correspondents appointed by the public sector banks and private sector banks at present are only 85 and 44 respectively. The number of accounts opened is 80.47 lakh by the public sector banks and 8.13 lakh by the private sector banks. While the Report has not prescribed any target for enlisting the new entities for appointment, its tone appears to be suggesting all out efforts to be made to reach out. This may turn out to be an overdose, if proper care is not taken in the selection process.

9 | Financial Inclusion

Looking Ahead

The government and the RBI have taken a number of initiatives to bring the financially excluded, underprivileged and weaker sections of the society within the fold of the formal financial system. These measures have, no doubt, some positive impact on financial inclusion. However, the magnitude of the problem and issues and challenges involved are enormous. Sill the majority of the rural and urban low income and poor segment of the population have very little or no access adequately to financial services from the formal financial system. Barriers to access both on demand-side and supply-side require to be removed to achieve greater financial inclusion. This chapter therefore seeks to go beyond the present state of financial inclusion and to chart out, based on the past achievement, strategies and an agenda for action to give a conscious thrust for achieving faster and sustainable financial inclusion in India.

Need for Integrated Planning

Planning at the district level under the lead bank scheme has been in operation for over three decades covering all districts in India. Passing through various stages of patronage and neglect, it has become a part of the banking operations at the branch level. Its acceptance at the macro level as a planning tool has not been, however, very explicit nor its utilisation as the base for sectoral credit targets at the policymakers' level. Yet it has been continued, partly as a ritualistic exercise repeated regularly by the district level functionaries. The annual publication of the *District Credit Plans* attracts media coverage, reminding the existence of the lead bank scheme. Over the years, it has become a form-filling exercise, making the district credit plans a bundle of data relating to branch-wise, scheme-wise, block-wise and bank-wise credit targets, both annual and quarterly.

The contribution made by the lead bank scheme in the initial stages cannot be underestimated in carrying banking to the unbanked villages. It has played a significant role in expanding the geographical spread of banking, especially into the unbanked and less banked rural areas all over the country. Over 30,000 villages could find a place in the banking map of the country as a result of the field surveys made by the lead banks. The branch managers were made to play the role of planners for preparing service area credit plans—an experiment, which perhaps has no parallels in the banking history anywhere in the world. A new group of lead district managers has emerged, undertaking pioneering work in rural banking, wherever the bank management supported them, implementing the lead bank scheme both in spirit and letters.

Today, when it is realised that even after 40 years of public sector banking, a large portion of the rural population still remains unreached by the banking system, there is an imperative need for reinventing the lead bank scheme (Thingalaya, 2009c). It requires careful planning and not ad hoc target fixation as some banks have started doing. It has to be built into the sectoral plans at the district level in the district credit plan. This is not being done in the present planning process.

Extension of financial support to the needy according to their requirements, at affordable price, repayable at convenient instalments is the ultimate goal. This cannot be achieved by listing them overnight as account holders; either through no-frills accounts or through small doses of credit in one go. This has to be based on a planned exercise, mapping the credit needs of individual households at the village level. The service area plans, as is being prepared at present is inadequate to undertake the credit mapping of individual households. The much-maligned district credit plan has to be rejuvenated and the lead district managers have to be reoriented towards this goal. A careful analysis of the Census 2001 data at the *taluk* level should be the starting point. Adding annually a few new accounts per branch is not the desirable route. It would be only an ad hoc patch work. What is needed is a solid roadmap.

There is a large scale proliferation of the self-help groups in many parts of the country. Signs of fatigue setting in many of them are slowly emerging. Multiple membership and cross-migration of members are taking place in certain cases. To avoid this, the promotion of SHGs should be made an integral part of the credit planning exercise at the village level, based on the actual need for them.

Financial inclusion should be the beginning of the mutually beneficial nexus between the banks and the households. The enthusiasm to reach out to the unreached should not result in increasing the dormant savings bank deposits after the initial drive vanishes. Nor should the easy access to institutional credit result in the borrowers bearing the debt burden involuntarily. Lead district managers should see beyond financial inclusion to forge a sustainable relationship between the banks and the households.

NABARD prepares the potential-linked plans (PLP) for every district. Similarly, the lead district managers prepare district credit plans (DCP) for all the districts, besides preparing annual credit plans. It is difficult to ascertain as to how they are actually used by the branch managers in preparing their service area credit plans for the villages allotted to them. NABARD has entered into the district planning arena, at a time, when it was felt that the banks were not having the necessary expertise. The PLP formulates the basic plan framework, while the DCP translates them into bank-wise and *taluk*-wise targets. If the two plans could be merged, the first part would have plan details and the second part would provide the credit targets for the banks operating in the district. NABARD may make a thorough review of the need for continuing the PLP in its present form.

Service area credit plan (SAP) prepared by the branch manager for the villages coming under his service area is based on an elaborately designed format. All the conceivable credit needs of the prospective borrowers in each village are built into it in the form of columns and rows to be meticulously filled in by the branch manager. It has 139 rows of detailed credit classifications and 20 columns, indicating physical and financial targets for each quarter. This format known as LBR 1U1 SAP has 2780 slots to be filled in. Adding to the work load of the branch managers, this format has more redundant columns than necessary. Hence, it is filled up ritualistically, with more blank slots than filled in slots. With all these details, it does not contain columns for the advances made to SHGs at the branch. Nor does it provide any indication of the plans for reaching out to prospective customers. The very size of the format is discouraging. The branch manager, besides his other office work, cannot find time to make quarterly review of SAP based on this elaborate format, more so, where the villages coming under his service area are more than one. In many cases, the number of villages varies from one to six covered by the service area of the branch.

There is an imperative need for revising this format, making it simpler and specific to the individual branches. This format has to be used for preparing the action plan of the branch to cover all the families in the service area over a period of time. This calls for specific survey of each household to assess their total banking needs. Currently, the credit targets are not based on actual assessment of the needs of each household. Mere addition of a few more columns to the SAP format is not desirable.

Clearly drafted manual of instructions is required to be prepared for making the planning exercise under the initiative of financial inclusion successful. Besides this, training the LDM is equally important. The College of Agricultural Banking of the Reserve Bank of India should have training programmes for the LDMs on a continuous basis. In view of the crucial role the LDMs are expected to play, the need for developing a cadre of LDMs may be examined. LDMs should be not less than the rank of scale IV officers, preferably with the qualification of post-graduates in economics or agricultural sciences.

Operationally, the success of the programme for financial inclusion would depend largely upon the involvement of the branch managers, manning the large number of rural branches scattered widely. While they are already involved in the preparation of service area plans with all its limitations, they need to be motivated to take up the challenge of financial inclusion. The task here is much more than mere data collection and preparing the annual plans. Creating an awareness in them about the philosophy of inclusive growth through training and rewarding the best performers are of crucial importance.

Financial Inclusion: A Roadmap

Financial inclusion is not an end in itself. It is one of the means for reaching out to all sections of the society for facilitating inclusive growth. The manner in which announcements are made about the achievement of hundred per cent financial inclusion, in a large number of districts within too short a period, leads to a state of complacency. There are multiple agencies engaged in formulating developmental plans at various levels, most of which are made in isolation, confining to a few selected issues or areas. Their integration at the district or state level is only an aggregation, which often has very little relevance to grassroot level needs or aspirations. Compartmentalisation of developmental initiatives combined with bureaucratic and political interventions render the planning process a ritual.

Bankers are drawn into this endless process of planning on paper, ever since the SAPs have been introduced under the lead bank scheme. Elaborate formats for data collection and review are prescribed to generate voluminous data at periodical intervals. Review meetings are held quarterly at different levels—block level, district level and state level. Voluminous district credit plan reports are prepared for over 600 districts containing enormous data. Copies are printed and circulated to all bank branches and their controlling offices besides the development departments at the district level. There is an imperative need for minimising the massive data collection and the resultant paper work.

The action points for attaining sustainable financial inclusion over a period, unfettered by arbitrary targets, involving many agencies having a stake in such a development are enumerated below.

Extending the Service Points

Identification of spatial gaps in the availability of banking facilities in each district, beginning with the most backward districts, should be the starting point. The lead bank has to identify the unbanked centres in each district, as was done in the 70s and 80s. More rural branches have to be opened, specially in the less banked districts. In other identified centres, virtual branches with business correspondents should be opened by the lead bank. Branchless banking model, with proper training of the business correspondent and proper safeguards built into the system should be the preferable mode for reaching out to larger households in a cost-effective manner.

Setting up *Gramin Vikas Soudhas*

Based on the logistics of the underbanked districts, a few central villages have to be selected for branch opening. Central villages are those villages, on which a good number of villages from the surrounding area depend for many of their marketing needs and for administrative purposes. The lead bank, in association with the local *panchayat* should put up a utilitarian building to house the new rural branch. Besides the branch, services facilities like, post office, primary health centre, ration shop and the *panchayat* office have to be located in this building. These branches should be computerised and work as nodal branches for business correspondents. A counseling centre also could be attached to such branches. All the developmental activities like the farm extension programmes, farmers' clubs, solar demonstration plants, adult education centre etc., could be added, depending upon the local needs.

If located in central villages, such centres can generate economic impulses contributing to the development of the surrounding villages also. Besides the demonstration effects, they have good publicity values also. Investments on these centres could be made by the lead banks, diverting a small portion of their publicity budget, if necessary.

Conducting Family Surveys

A simplified format has to be designed by revising the present service area plan format for collecting the basic data pertaining to each household in the villages coming under the service of each branch. Besides the branch managers, the business correspondents also should be trained to gather the relevant data relating to the expectations of each adult member of the households. The respondents have to be educated about the banking transactions and the pros and cons of borrowing from the bank. Benchmark data for all the households have to be prepared and stored at the LDMs' offices to be updated, whenever changes in their economic status are reported by the branch managers.

Integrating Credit Plan with Developmental Plans

Performance budgeting exercise, which each branch was doing in the past to formulate annually its own branch plan should be revived for credit mapping the households. The branch manager has to prepare the village level credit plan by consolidating household credit plans. Integrating the village credit plan with the developmental plan of the village *panchayat*, if any, and dovetail it with the block level developmental plans. The village plans have to be finalised in consultation with the lead district manager, taking cognition of any of the major development projects expected to be implemented in the village.

Reorienting the Lead District Manager

Supervising the formulation of village credit plan has to be done by LDM, assisting the branch manager in seeking the cooperation of block level staff. He has to ensure that all branch managers prepare the credit plans for the villages in their service area. He has to look into the need for realigning the service areas, where necessary in consultation with the banks concerned.

Posting the right type of staff as LDMs and to train them in-house or at other training centres like College of Agricultural Banking (CAB) or National Institute of Bank Management (NIBM) is an important step for the successful completion of the process of financial inclusion. Once the whole plan is prepared, the functional departments at the controlling offices should sanction the proposals emanating from the branches based on the integrated village plans.

No arbitrary targets should be imposed on the branches once their plans are approved. Any addition to credit deployment and creation of required facilities at the branch level should be within the plan. Promotion and close monitoring of the functioning of SHGs should be done by the LDMs.

Involving Other Financial Agencies

Since banking industry is one of the many agencies providing financial services and selling financial products, it would be desirable to include some of the other segments of the financial sector in attaining financial inclusion. Cooperative banks, insurance companies, self-help groups and microfinance institutions are the important agencies, which can play a complementary role. Life Insurance Corporation (LIC) of India, in fact had a programme called *Bima Gram*, identifying villages having over 75 per cent of the eligible persons in the village having life insurance policies. Such villages are given financial support for setting up community projects. At present in addition to LIC, there are many other insurance companies in the private sector. Self-help groups are also reaching out to growing number of households. Microfinance institutions are proliferating. Cooperative sector has its own clientele, both active and passive. Private sector banks are slowly entering into the rural sector. Mention may be also made of housing finance companies as well as mutual fund companies, both in the private and public sectors. Though their presence is more in urban India than in rural areas at present, they are extending their operations into rural areas also.

There is hardly any coordination among these financial agencies and the banks as far as their involvement in attaining financial inclusion is concerned. Normally those who have insurance also have savings bank accounts, so also in the case of the customers of mutual funds and housing companies. However, there is no mechanism in place to provide a comprehensive picture of the penetration of all these agencies in the financial activities at the district level. It is desirable that the lead district manager should be made the nodal officer to collect annually the relevant data from these agencies at the district level as a supplement to the plan for financial inclusion.

Reserve Bank of India to Redraw the Target Date

For all those who have a stake in making financial inclusion a success, it would be more prudent to accept the proposition that hundred per cent financial inclusion in the real sense cannot be achieved, in a couple of years. The achievement could be made in a staggered manner with a time horizon dictated by the specific local conditions, specially in an economy like ours, known for its geographical and socioeconomic diversities.

It would be highly desirable that the Reserve Bank of India should not impose any short-term targets for reaching out to the entire population. Banks may be discouraged from claiming too often the hundred per cent coverage of districts in large number. Instead of fixing the target date for total coverage by 2015 as recommended by Dr. Rangarajan Committee, it may be extended to 2019, the year in which public sector banks in India would be celebrating their golden jubilee.

In order to reach this goal, the service points have to be expanded substantially. Banks may be directed to identify the unbanked centres for opening new branches, as they have done in the 70s. The branch licensing policy may be modified to hasten the process of rural branch expansion specially in those districts, where the financial coverage is very poor at present.

Persuading the Government of India

The Census of India 2001 has in fact made the first comprehensive study of financial inclusion by enumerating the number of households having bank accounts in its *Analytical Report on Household Assets*. The detailed database for all districts and *taluks* in India are enumerated for rural and urban households. Surprisingly, none of the reports or circulars of the Reserve Bank of India makes any reference to this benchmark data.

As the preparations for 2011 Census have already begun, the census authorities may be advised by the Government of India to continue to enumerate this data in the forthcoming census enumeration. They may be persuaded to seek a few more details from the households than merely asking whether any member of the household has a bank account. This question may be enlarged to seek the details of all members of the household having or not having bank accounts. From this enumeration, authentic data of banking penetration for all the districts and *taluks* in India would be available by 2015. Based on this data, the necessary corrective actions could be taken in the districts lagging behind, so as to complete the process by 2019, the proposed target date.

Innovative Inclusion

Instead of confining to the schemes recommended by the official committees, banks may adopt some innovative schemes for making financial inclusion more meaningful as well as successful. In a write up, "Financial Inclusion: A FAB Idea", published in *The Economist*, quoting Prof. Bhagwan Chowdhry of the University of California, a suggestion is made for giving every new born child an online bank account with $100 in it. The aim of Financial Access @Birth (FAB) is to provide financial help to the poor children in their infancy. It is observed that half the world's population has no bank account and hence catching them young would be very beneficial to them (*The Economist*, 2010).

Taking a clue from this scheme of thinking, it is suggested that in India, every branch of the banks may credit Rs.1000 to the account of the child born within their service area. A fixed deposit account may be opened in the joint names of the father or mother and the child. It could be for a period of 15 years, till the child completes high school education. If such long term depositing does not fit into the permissible banking practice, the deposit could be made initially for a period of five years and renewed with interest for the next five years twice. In this process, the parents also become bank customers besides the new born child.

The banks should not have difficulties in ear-marking a portion of their net profit for this purpose annually. If 10 per cent of the annual expenditure on advertisement could be diverted for this purpose, they can create the deposit accounts of all the new born children in the branches of their lead districts. Instead of making film actors or sportsmen as their brand ambassadors at huge cost, those funds can be fruitfully used for this purpose.

An experiment of this type was made by the Government of Karnataka in the early 90s to provide an incentive for the school children to improve their school attendance. Banks in the state were directed to open savings bank accounts in the name of all the school going children. The head masters of the schools were asked to credit one rupee for each day's attendance at the end of the month. Based on the recommendation of school, the branch manager would credit the amount to the individual savings accounts at the end of the month and then obtain reimbursement from the state government. Large number of savings bank accounts was opened by the bank branches, when branches were not computerised. This worked well for sometime improving the school attendance. However, since the savings accounts were in the name of the parents, the amounts were withdrawn periodically by the indebted father and ultimately the scheme became defunct. Some procedural safeguards have to be incorporated to make the new scheme really useful to the children. The deposit should be made as a fixed deposit not eligible for premature withdrawal except in case of death of the child.

Nearly a century ago, the Royal Commission on Indian Agriculture appointed by the British government has made a rhetoric statement, "Indian farmer is born in debt, lives in debt and dies in debt" (Government of India, 1927). The members of this Commission may turn in their graves, when they hear that the Indian farmer's new born child enters the world now with a deposit to his credit, if not a silver spoon in his mouth. Financial inclusion would be certainly meaningful if a scheme like this is adopted by the banking sector in India.

In the final analysis, the study of financial inclusion should not end in a mere statistical exercise. It should emerge as a means for facilitating the inclusive growth of all sections of the society. It is not the responsibility of the banking sector alone in achieving this ideal goal. Necessarily it has to be based on collective efforts.

As Gandhiji has pleaded, "Remember that dark brown starved man, bending under a scorching sun, scratching a little plot of land to eke out a living..... anything you do, do for his benefit."

Bibliography and References

Agarwal, Gaurav (2007). "Financial Inclusion through Mobile Phone Banking: Issues and Challenges", *CAB Calling*, July–September, Pune.

Asian Development Bank (2000). *Finance for the Poor: Micro-finance Development Strategy*, Manila.

———. (2007). "Low Income Households' Access to Financial Services International Experience, Measures for Improvement and the Future", *EARD Special Studies*. October.

Bank of Scotland (2005). *Delivering Our Financial Inclusion Agenda*.

Beck, T.A., Demirguc-Kunt, M. Soledad and M. Peria (2007). "Reaching Out: Access to and Use of Banking Services across Countries", *Journal of Financial Economics* 85(1).

Carbo, S., E.P.M. Gardener and P. Molyneux (2005). *Financial Exclusion*. Palgrave MacMillan.

Census of India (2008). *Analytical Report on Household Assets*. Census 2001, New Delhi.

Chant Link and Associates (2004). *A Report on Financial Exclusion in Australia*. November.

Claessens, Stijn (2006). "Access to Financial Services: A Review of the Issues and Public Policy Objectives", *World Bank Research Observer* 21(2). Washington D.C.: The World Bank.

Connolly, C. and K. Hajaj (2001). *Financial Services and Social Exclusion*. University of New South Wales: Financial Services Consumer Policy Centre.

Easton, Tom (2005). "The Hidden Wealth of the Poor", in *The Economist*, November 5, London.

Ford, J. and K. Rowlingson (1996). "Low-Income Households and Credit Exclusion, Preferences and Inclusion", *Environment and Planning* 28: 1345-60.

Government of India (1927): *Report of the Royal Commission on Indian Agriculture*, New Delhi.

Government of India (2008). *Report of the Committee on Financial Inclusion* (Rangarajan Committee). New Delhi: Government of India.

———. (2008). *Eleventh Five Year Plan: 2007-2012*, Vol. I: Inclusive Growth, Planning Commission, New Delhi.

———. (2007). *Report of the Working Group on Competitive Micro-credit Market in India*. Eleventh Five Year Plan, Planning Commission, New Delhi.

———. (2005). *Census of India 2001: Analytical Report on Household Assets*. New Delhi.

H.M. Treasury Committee (2006). "Financial Inclusion: Credit, Savings, Advice and Insurance, Twelfth Report of Session 2005-06", Vol.1. U.K.: House of Commons Treasury Committee.

Treasury, H.M. (2004). *Promoting Financial Inclusion*, HIMSO. 2:16 Colgate, Norwich, U.K.

————. (2007). *Financial Inclusion: The Way Forward*. London.

Indian Institute of Banking & Finance (2006). *Readings on Financial Inclusion*. New Delhi: Taxman Publications Pvt.Ltd.

IIMS (2007). *Invest India Incomes and Savings Survey*, Invest India Market Solutions.

Kamath, Raghav (2007). "Branchless Banking: Corp. Bank's Answer for Financial Inclusion", *CAB Calling* 31(3), July-September.

Kempson, E. (2006). "Policy Level Response to Financial Exclusion in Developed Economies: Lessons for Developing Countries", *Paper for Access to Finance: Building Inclusive Financial Systems*. Washington D.C.: World Bank.

Kempson, Elaine, Claire Whyley, John Caskey and Sharon Collard (2000). *In or Out? Financial Exclusion: A Literature and Research Review*. London: Financial Services Authority.

Leeladhar, V. (2006). "Taking Banking Services to the Common Man—Financial Inclusion", *RBI Bulletin*, January, Mumbai.

Leyshon, A. and N. Thrift (1993). "The Restructuring of the UK Financial Services Industry in the 1990s: A Reversal of Fortune?", *Journal of Rural Studies* 9: 223-41.

————. (1995). "Geographies of Financial Exclusion: Financial Abandonment in Britain and United States", *Transaction of the Institute of British Geographers*, New Series 20: 312-41.

Meadows, P., P. Ormerod and W. Cook (2004). "Social Networks: Their Role in Access to Financial Services in Britain", *National Institute Economic Review* (189): 99-109.

Mujumdar, N.A. (2007). *Inclusive Growth—Development Perspectives in Indian Economy*. New Delhi: Academic Foundation.

Mohan, Rakesh (2006). "Economic Growth, Financial Deepening and Financial Exclusion", *RBI Bulletin*, November, Mumbai.

Moodithaya, M.S. (2009). *Rural Self-Employment Programmes in India: An Appraisal*. New Delhi: Manak Publications Pvt. Ltd.

NABARD (1999). *Report of RBI's Working Group on Non-Governmental Organizations and Self-Help Groups*, Mumbai.

————. (1999). *Report of The Task Force on Supportive Policy and Regulatory Framework for Microfinance*, Mumbai.

————. (2009). *Financial Inclusion–An Overview, Department of Economic Analysis and Research*. Mumbai: NABARD.

NCAER (2008). *How India Earns, Spends and Saves*, The Max New York Life-NCAER India Financial Protection Survey, New Delhi.

Otero, Maria and Rhyne Elisabeth (1994). *The New World of Micro-Enterprise Finance*. Connecticut, U.S.A.: Kumarian Press.

Rangarajan, C (2008). *Report of the Committee on Financial Inclusion in India*. New Delhi: Government of India.

Reserve Bank of India (1956). *Report of the All India Rural Credit Survey*. Mumbai.

————. (1969). "Organisational Framework for the Implementation of Social Objectives", in *Reserve Bank of India Bulletin*, November. Mumbai

————. (2006). *Basic Statistical Returns of Scheduled Commercial Banks in India*, Volume 35, March. Mumbai.

————. (2007). *Basic Statistical Returns of Scheduled Commercial Banks in India*, Volume 36, March, Mumbai.

————. (2008). *Reports on Currency and Finance 2003-08, Vol.V, The Banking Sector in India: Emerging Issues and Challenges, Chapter VII: Financial Inclusion*, Mumbai.

————. (2009). *Report of the High Level Committee to Review the Lead Bank Scheme*. Mumbai.

Robinson, Marguerite (2001). *The Microfinance Revolution: Sustainable Banking for the Poor*. Washington D.C.: The World Bank.

Sinclair, Stephen P. (2001). *Financial Exclusion: An Introductory Survey*. Heriot Watt University: Centre for Research into Socially Inclusive Services(CRSIS).

Stiglitz, Joseph and Andrew Weiss (1981). "Credit Rationing in Markets with Imperfect Information", *American Economic Review* 71(3): 393-410.

Shetty, N.S. (2008). "Global Financial Melt-Down: Whither India?", *Nitte Management Review* 2(2). December. Nitte.

The Economist (2010). "Financial Inclusion: A FAB Idea", March 6, 2010, London.

Thingalaya, N.K. (1997). *Banking Development in Independent India*. Manipal: Syndicate Bank.

————. (2000). *The Other side of Rural Banking*. Lucknow: Bankers' Institute of Rural Development.

————. (2001). "The Millennium Count", *Business India*, September 7-20, Mumbai.

————. (2005). "Tiny Deposits: Rising from the Bottom of the Pyramid", in *Industrial Economist*, April 30, Chennai.

————. (2007). "Branchless Banking: The New Trend", *Industrial Economist*, December, Chennai.

————. (2008). "Banking in Puducherry: Slow Growth", *Industrial Economist*, December, Chennai.

————. (2009a). "Financial Inclusion: The Effectiveness of No-Frills Accounts", in *Industrial Economist*. Chennai, April.

————. (2009b). *Banks in the South: Past, Present and Their Future*. Nitte: Justice K.S. Hegde Institute of Management.

————. (2009c). "Forty Years of Public Sector Banking", in *Industrial Economist*, August, Chennai.

————. (2009d). "Banking Penetration: Still Poor", in *Industrial Economist*, November, Chennai.

————. (2002). "Relevance of Regional Rural Banks", paper presented at *IRMA Silver Jubilee Symposium*, Anand. (Volume yet to be published).

Thingalaya, N.K., N.S. Shetty and M.S. Moodithaya (2004). "Microfinance and Rural Employment: An Appraisal of the Potentialities", *Research Report* submitted to NABARD, J.K.S.H. Institute of Management, Nitte.

Thorat, Usha (2008). "Financial Inclusion and Information Technology", *RBI Bulletin*, October, Mumbai.

————. (2006). "Financial Inclusion and Millennium Development Goals", *RBI Bulletin*, February, Mumbai.

United Nations (2006). *Building Inclusive Financial Sectors for Development*. New York.

World Bank (2004). *India: Scaling Up Access to Finance for India's Rural Poor.* Washington, D.C.

————. (2008). *Finance for All? Policies and Pitfalls in Expanding Access.* Washington, D.C.

Reports

Andhra Pragathi Grameena Bank (2009). *Annual Report 2008-09*, Kadapa.

Canara Bank (2009). *Annual Report 2008-09*, Bangalore.

Corporation Bank (2009). *Annual Report 2008-09*, Mangalore.

Gurgaon Gramin Bank (2009). *Annual Report 2008-09*, Gurgaon.

Indian Bank (2009). *Annual Report 2008-09*, Chennai.

Indian Overseas Bank (2009). *Annual Report 2008-09*, Chennai.

Karnataka Vikas Grameena Bank (2009). *Annual Report 2008-09*, Dharwad.

North Malabar Gramin Bank (2009). *33rd Annual Report 2008-09*, Kannur.

Pandyan Grama Bank (2008). *Annual Report 2007-08*, Virudhnagar.

Reserve Bank of India (2009). *Annual Policy Statement for the Year 2009-10*, Mumbai.

Reserve Bank of India (2005). *Report of the Internal Group to Examine Issues Relating to Rural Credit and Microfinance*, Mumbai.

Reserve Bank of India (2009). *Report of the Working Group to Review the Business Correspondent Model*, Mumbai.

South Malabar Gramin Bank (2009). *Annual Report 2008-09*, Malappuram.

State Bank of Hyderabad (2009). *Annual Report 2008-09*, Hyderabad.

State Bank of Travancore (2009). *Annual Report 2008-09*, Thiruvanathapuram.

Syndicate Bank (2009). *Annual Report 2008-09*, Bangalore.

Vijaya Bank (2009). *Annual Report 2008-09*, Bangalore.

Annexures

Annexure A-1

Number of Households Availing Banking Services

States	Households (in lakh)			Percentage		
	Rural	Urban	Total	Rural	Urban	Total
Andhra Pradesh	38.50	13.79	52.29	30.37	33.04	31.03
Arunachal Pradesh	0.47	0.32	0.79	28.65	66.67	37.26
Assam	6.32	3.81	10.13	14.97	53.28	20.52
Bihar	23.60	6.24	29.84	18.64	47.20	21.34
Chhattisgarh	6.35	3.65	10.00	18.87	46.26	24.10
Goa	0.97	1.06	2.03	23.71	76.81	72.76
Gujarat	17.58	18.91	36.49	29.85	50.32	37.83
Haryana	10.41	5.55	15.96	42.42	51.62	45.22
Himachal Pradesh	6.31	1.07	7.38	57.52	74.82	59.51
Jammu & Kashmir	3.45	2.21	5.66	29.62	56.56	36.43
Jharkhand	8.06	6.59	14.65	21.20	62.17	30.13
Karnataka	23.50	17.42	40.92	35.20	48.93	40.00
Kerala	24.79	8.91	33.70	50.16	53.93	51.09
Madhya Pradesh	17.14	13.34	30.48	21.10	47.74	27.92
Maharashtra	43.33	48.42	91.75	39.41	60.01	48.13
Manipur	0.19	0.16	0.35	6.08	15.84	8.81
Meghalaya	0.42	0.46	0.88	12.76	50.36	20.71
Mizoram	0.13	0.38	0.51	16.45	46.91	31.67
Nagaland	0.31	0.22	0.53	11.32	32.83	15.96
Orissa	13.39	5.66	19.05	19.74	52.06	24.20
Puducherry	0.18	0.48	0.66	23.61	35.29	31.73
Punjab	12.69	7.99	20.68	45.72	54.76	48.48
Rajasthan	17.16	9.83	26.99	23.98	44.94	28.89
Sikkim	0.23	0.08	0.31	24.17	61.53	29.80
Tamil Nadu	14.65	17.70	32.35	17.70	30.00	22.82
Tripura	1.11	0.64	1.75	20.59	51.64	26.43
Uttar Pradesh	86.27	27.38	113.65	41.89	52.95	44.18
Uttarakhand	6.71	2.77	9.48	56.10	71.02	59.77
West Bengal	30.76	27.05	57.81	27.55	59.39	36.77
All-India	416.40	265.90	682.30	30.11	49.52	35.54

Source: Census of India–2001, H-Series.

Annexure A-2

Gramin Banks in the Southern States: March 2009

State	*Name of Gramin Bank*	*Location*	*Sponsoring Bank*
Andhra Pradesh	Saptagiri Grameena Bank	Chittoor	Indian Bank
	Chaitanya Godavari Grameena Bank	Guntur	Andhra Bank
	Andhra Pragathi Grameena Bank	Kadapa	Syndicate Bank
	Andhra Pradesh Grameena Vikas Bank	Warangal	State Bank of India
	Deccan Grameena Bank	Hyderabad	State Bank of Hyderabad
Karnataka	Pragathi Gramin Bank	Bellary	Canara Bank
	Karnataka Vikas Grameena Bank	Dharwad	Syndicate Bank
	Cauvery Kalpatharu Grameena Bank	Mysore	State Bank of Mysore
	Visveshvaraya Gramin Bank	Mandya	Vijaya Bank
	Krishna Grameena Bank	Gulbarga	State Bank of India
	Chikmagalur-Kodagu Grameena Bank	Chikmagalur	Corporation Bank
Kerala	North Malabar Gramin Bank	Kannur	Syndicate Bank
	South Malabar Gramin Bank	Malappuram	Canara Bank
Tamil Nadu	Pallavan Grama Bank	Salem	Indian Bank
	Pandyan Grama Bank	Virudhnagar	Indian Overseas Bank

Source: Thingalaya, N.K. *Gramin Banks Bounce Back* published by Justice K.S. Hegde Institute of Management, Nitte. March 2010.